NOTRE DAME

Where Have You Gone?

Eric Hansen

www.SportsPublishingLLC.com

ISBN: 1-58261-151-3

Publishers: Peter L. Bannon and Joseph J. Bannon Sr.
Senior managing editor: Susan M. Moyer
Acquisitions editor: Mike Pearson
Developmental editor: Noah Adams Amstadter
Art director: K. Jeffrey Higgerson
Dust jacket design: Joseph Brumleve
Interior layout: Kathryn R. Holleman
Imaging: Kayte Holleman, Dustin Hubbart, and Heidi Norsen
Photo editor: Erin Linden-Levy
Vice president of sales and marketing: Kevin King
Media and promotions managers: Courtney Hainline (regional),
        Randy Fouts (national), Maurey Williamson (print)

Printed in the United States of America

Sports Publishing L.L.C.
804 North Neil Street
Champaign, IL 61820

Phone: 1-877-424-2665
Fax: 217-363-2073
www.SportsPublishingLLC.com

*To my sons, Antonio and Blake,
and to my grandma, Nona Mary Fatibeno,
whose strength and conviction opened doors to
dreams for all of us*

CONTENTS

ACKNOWLEDGMENTS

I would first like to thank the former Notre Dame players who made this project possible, for their stories, for their candor, for their time.

To Noah Amstadter at Sports Publishing LLC, for all his great ideas, for being a great collaborator, for his patience with our flighty e-mail system and for thinking of me for this project in the first place. I'd like to thank Mike Pearson at Sports Publishing for his vision as well.

To Bill Bilinski, the sports editor at the *South Bend Tribune*, whose support and understanding allow me to tackle projects like this. Bill, you're the best in the business and an even better person.

To my sons, Blake and Antonio, who sacrificed hours of potential instant message time with the girls at their respective schools so that Dad could use the computer.

To photographer Joe Raymond, whose help was invaluable with the photos and whose own athletic career ended somewhat tragically at the Newman Center House of Pain.

To co-workers Bob Wieneke and Jason Kelly at the *South Bend Tribune* and *Irish Sports Report*, who helped me with numbers, gave me feedback and put up with my moods—and both of whom "get it."

To Bob Hammel, who has been in my corner from the time I walked into this business, thank you for always being there for me.

To Doug Walker, who does much more than provide veggie pitas for hungry sports writers in his capacity as associate sports information director at Notre Dame. He is also the best in his field. I'd also like to thank Susan McGonigal for her help with the phone numbers. To Carol Copley, the happiest person on this planet, and to John Heisler for their help in tracking down photos.

To my mother, Celia Hansen, and my aunt, Linda Koplin, for their encouragement and support.

To *Chicago Tribune* writer David Haugh, who was always there to bounce ideas off of and whose power to decipher my long-winded, cryptic e-mails was a huge help.

To Vicki Bishop, my 10th-grade English teacher at Northland High, and Sharon West, a journalism professor at the Ohio State University—two teachers who made a difference.

To Sandy Schwartz, who gave me my start in this business.

To my friends, David George, Michael Settonni, and Pearson Buell, for believing in me.

To Vaughn McClure, a rising star in the journalism business, the one person I know who must have at least two mobile phones at all times and a man who doesn't mind a late-night phone call—even if you'll eventually end up on "call waiting."

I want to thank the guy upstairs—for everything.

And finally to my father, the late Alf Holter Hansen, a Norwegian immigrant, who unselfishly sacrificed everything so that his son could follow his dreams. I want to acknowledge him and thank him for that. I'm not sure if there are bookstores in heaven, but if there are, my dad is smiling bigger than anyone else up there today.

INTRODUCTION

It doesn't always start with a dream, but somewhere along the way the Notre Dame experience seems to engender one.

It's what remains after the cheering stops. It's the imprint that ties All-Americans like Ken MacAfee, Derrick Mayes, and Ned Bolcar with walk-ons like Matt Sarb. It's what coaxes a player like Troy Ridgley, who gouged his football potential with poor decisions before finally being expelled, to want to come back to Notre Dame years later—and to give back.

It's what helps a player like Greg Davis, known for committing the clip on Rocket Ismail's punt return, or Jim Sanson, whose kicking miscues gave rise to death threats, transcend the moment and go on to make a difference in the real world.

It can be as simple as appreciating your parents' sacrifices and growing into the man they'd always hoped you'd become, like Jerome Heavens, or as complex as trying to rebuild homes and lives amidst a corrupt government, nightmarish logistics and a sea of apathy in tsunami-torn Sri Lanka, like Aaron Taylor.

It is something you can't buy in the campus bookstore or capture in a snapshot of Touchdown Jesus or even read in a football box score. Yet the Notre Dame experience—the unyielding spirit and the struggle—is as tangible as it is ethereal. You can see it in Pete Duranko's smile as he bravely battles incurable ALS (Lou Gehrig's Disease). You can hear it in the songs composed by John Scully. You can feel it every time special education teacher Nick Eddy makes a difference with a kid someone else had given up on.

It is the inspiration for this book, *Notre Dame: Where Have You Gone?*

On the following pages, we will not only catch up with 37 former Fighting Irish football players, we will gain understanding of what pulled them to Notre Dame and, in some instances, what kept them there through waves of adversity.

We will also see what lives touched theirs and vice versa, for better or for worse. Through the eyes of Mike Larkin and Bob Crable, two players who played for Gerry Faust at Cincinnati Moeller High School and at Notre Dame, we glean insight into why the Faust experience at Notre Dame didn't work in South Bend.

Through players like Bolcar, Pete Bercich, Pat Terrell and Pat Eilers, we see why Lou Holtz was so tough to play for, but also why he was so revered—especially when those players found out how willing Holtz was to be a part of their lives after football.

Through MacAfee we see that Dan Devine succeeded by surrounding himself with great people and by staying out of their way. From Coley O'Brien, Rocky Bleier, Eddy and Duranko, we can see the genius and the compassion of Ara Parseghian.

Through Bercich and Steve Orsini, we gain a better understanding of what deposed coach George O'Leary was about and what might have been had he stayed at Notre Dame longer than five days.

We'll look at coaching changes that were empowering and those that tested the players' resolve. We'll look at notable moments in Irish football—Robin Weber's catch, Ivory Covington's tackle, Rusty Lisch's being replaced at quarterback by Joe Montana—and how those players frame those experiences years later.

The "Where Are They Now?" genre of writing has always been a favorite of mine. I've always been curious how players transitioned into post-football life, whether they were able to apply the lessons they learned in college on and off the field, and whether they transcended the touchdowns as well as the fumbles years later.

What makes the Notre Dame group all the more intriguing against this backdrop are the common threads—the sense of home and belonging, the enduring passion and strength—that came from their time at Notre Dame, even if their time in South Bend was truncated by a transfer, an injury, or an expulsion.

The dreams are born and the dreams continue, even though they don't look the same. The spirit is what has driven Notre Dame to produce an unprecedented seven Heisman Trophy winners, build one of the most impressive won-loss records in the history of college football, attract its own TV network, and survive poor coaching cycles—not the other way around.

The statistics, the championships, the great upsets, the biting disappointments will always be a part of their lives, but it is the dreams that sprouted in and around those moments that will define them forever.

PETE BERCICH

P ete Bercich can't remember anymore how many weeks passed before he finally started sleeping through the night again. Or how many months it took before the sick feeling in the pit of his stomach finally went away.

"Some people are remembered for what they do," said Bercich, a former Notre Dame linebacker in the early '90s. "Some people are remembered for what they *didn't* do. And whatever category you fall in, there will always be people around to remind you of it—even years later. I still get razzed about it."

No one, though, was harder on Bercich for a dropped interception in the closing moments of Boston College's 41-39 upset of the No. 1-ranked Irish in the 1993 regular-season finale than Bercich himself. Even though there was a multitude of other plays that were just as significant, if not more, in the 16th-ranked Eagles' ambush. Even though he paved the way for an Irish Cotton Bowl victory over Texas A&M weeks later with, ironically, a fourth-quarter interception.

He couldn't move past it.

Not after the Minnesota Vikings made him a seventh-round draft choice that spring. Not when he made the Vikings' practice squad the next fall.

But it wasn't just the Boston College game. That was just the punctuation mark on a general malaise that had been building inside of Bercich for more than a year.

"Even before that game, I always felt like I was walking on eggshells," Bercich said. "There was no room for error. There was no fun left in football. It really had become burdensome. I remember my first day in Vikings mini-camp my rookie year. The next morning I woke up and looked in the mirror and said,

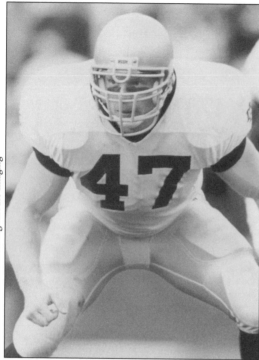

Michael and Susan Bennett/Lighthouse Imaging

Courtesy of the Minnesota Vikings

#47

PETE
BERCICH

LINEBACKER

PLAYING YEARS:
1990-1993

CLAIM TO FAME:
Dropped a potential
interception late in No.
1 Notre Dame's 41-39
loss to Boston College
in 1993, then came
back weeks later to pick
off a fourth-quarter
pass to preserve Notre
Dame's 24-21 Cotton
Bowl victory over Texas
A&M

HIGH SCHOOL:
Providence High
(New Lenox, Illinois)

HOMETOWN:
Mokena, Illinois

PROFESSION:
Linebackers coach for
the NFL's Minnesota
Vikings

**CURRENTLY RESIDES
IN:**
Lakeville, Minnesota

'You know what, if they cut me, I wouldn't be all that upset.' I had my degree, and I would have been ready to move on with my life."

Instead he stuck with the Vikings for seven years as a professional football player, six of those years on the active roster. And he fell in love with football all over again—so much so that he took up coaching for a living and is an ascending fourth-year assistant on Mike Tice's staff.

"When I was at Notre Dame, coaching was the last thing in the world I thought I'd end up doing," said Bercich, promoted from assistant linebackers coach to linebackers coach after the 2004 season. "I wanted to get into the FBI or the CIA. And Digger Phelps actually tried to help me out that way, but they weren't hiring at the time, so that kind of went by the wayside. I also thought about the financial world. But coaching? Never. It's funny how life is."

And Bercich, a husband and father of three young children, can laugh now. Laugh at those horrible things he thought about Irish head coach Lou Holtz when Bercich was playing college ball. Laugh about the pressures. Laugh about the fact he was so wrapped up in football and schoolwork at Notre Dame that he was too busy to realize he supposedly had no social life.

Suddenly, one day, everything made sense, though. Even the darkness.

"When you get recruited and you decide to go to Notre Dame, you're excited about it and you love it," Bercich said. "And when you were there, you hated it, because it was a tough place to go to school, and Lou was not an easy person to play for. When we were there, we always had a joke that the best view of the Golden Dome was the one in the rearview mirror. But once you leave, you appreciate it. You really do. And if I could do it all over again, I'd do the exact same thing."

Bercich's road to Notre Dame began near Joliet, Illinois. He actually grew up just east of the blue-collar city that has produced a disproportionate number of Division I college football players and America's most famous walk-on—Rudy. But instead of going to renowned football power Joliet Catholic, Bercich matriculated to Providence, a Catholic High School in New Lenox, Illinois, known more for its baseball program.

"I caught a lot of hell from some of my friends," Bercich said. "Some of them went to Joliet Catholic. Some of them went to the public school near me, Lincoln Way, but I think if there was one decision in my life that I made that changed my life—even more than my college decision—it was this one, to go to Providence. I had great coaches. I was around great people. I went to a place where you had to toe the line—dress codes and things like that. And so it got me prepared for my life more than anything else."

There was no question in Bercich's mind he was physically ready for a life in pro football when the time came, whether his heart was in it or not.

"The draft was the hardest part, going in the seventh round," he said. "I saw guys go in front of me I thought I was better than, and people kept telling me I was a long shot. It just never felt like that. Part of it may have been the fact my dad played pro football (Bob Bercich was a safety with the Dallas Cowboys in the early '60s.)

"When you grow up and your dad does something, you always think, 'If he can do it, I can do it.' So playing in the NFL wasn't a big deal in my house. That kind of took the edge off. The other thing was my parents really didn't keep me on a tight leash. They kind of let me be my own person, and I learned to make decisions, big decisions, at an early age. The only thing my parents wouldn't let me do was go to the University of Miami."

He didn't need advice from his parents when it came time to ponder the end of his football career. Injuries in 1999 and 2000 and a trip to the waiver wire were strong enough hints for Bercich that it was time to do something else with his life once the 2000 season came to a close. Dennis Green, the Vikings' head coach at that time, had once told Bercich that he showed great potential as a coach. But when Bercich asked Green for a chance to break into the business, Green could only offer more encouragement. There were no job openings.

Bercich spent the next nine months working for Bremen Castings, a foundry located 20 miles southeast of South Bend, and loved every minute of working in the company's interior sales department.

Green was fired near the end of the 2001 season, and Tice, then an assistant, took over on an interim basis. Once the "interim" tag was removed after the season, Tice offered Bercich a chance to join his staff.

"The hardest part of NFL coaching is getting in the door," Bercich said. "It's more about who you know than what you know. Still, it was a tough decision. South Bend was close to both of our families. And we knew that the lifestyle would be tough on my wife, especially as our family grew. She juggles being a mom and a dad. During the season, you have a very rigid schedule. I love my job, but [the long hours] that's the one thing that's not good. My wife, though, is very supportive."

Bercich has moved up quickly from defensive assistant/quality control to assistant linebackers coach to full-fledged linebackers coach.

Along the way, he has had the opportunity to scout and evaluate NFL Draft hopefuls from all over the country for the Vikings, including prospects for his alma mater.

"I don't doubt for a second that the talent level has fallen off some at Notre Dame," he said. "I don't see the speed across the board that we used to have when I played. They're still getting some talented players, just not as many of them. The depth of talent isn't there. That's the main thing."

There has been no shortage of talent, though, among the coaches Bercich has been exposed to. Among them was Green, who helped him rediscover his passion for football. In Tice, who put Bercich on a steep learning curve. In Holtz, who taught Bercich valuable life lessons. And in former Vikings assistant George O'Leary, who shared a dream with Bercich.

"We were talking about dream jobs one day," Bercich said of O'Leary. "I surprised him when I told him mine would be to return to Notre Dame someday as head coach. And he said, 'That was my dream too, and I lost it.'"

O'Leary was Notre Dame's head football coach for less than a week in December of 2001. He landed with Minnesota Vikings after his embellished bio led to his resignation and made him a national punch line in the sports world for a while. O'Leary coached the defensive line at Minnesota in 2002, then was promoted to defensive coordinator in 2003. He left the Vikings after the 2003 season to take the head coaching job at the University of Central Florida.

"Working with George was great," Bercich said. "He's a very disciplined guy, a very attention-to-detail guy. I think it's a shame that it didn't work out at Notre Dame, because I think he would have done a fantastic job. He'd have been a perfect fit. I think the attitude and toughness he brought would have been perfect.

"He's one of the reasons I say I've been blessed. I think the reason I'm in coaching is because I've been fortunate enough to have had great coaches all throughout my career. I've also played with some great players. I'm a product of who I've been with. There's a saying that goes, 'If I can see farther, it's because I've stood on the shoulders of giants.' That's kind of where I am in life now."

ROCKY BLEIER

I t was a career that almost ended before it got started.

Rocky Bleier can't remember what he talked about that less-than-memorable evening four decades ago, or where he was or even how many people were in the audience to hear the then-Notre Dame football captain speak.

But he does recall vividly how dry his mouth was and how fast his heart raced.

"I had never been that scared in all my life," Bleier said, laughing heartily at the mental imagery of him tripping over his words.

Today, Bleier makes a living telling his story to audiences all over the country, making roughly 80 to 105 speeches a year. He is married for the second time, with two adult children and three grandchildren. He also has two young daughters, ages six and seven, whom he and his second wife adopted from an orphanage in the Ukraine. Ironically, he met his second wife just after giving one of his speeches.

"I'll be honest, I hoped and I thought my speaking days were over after Notre Dame," said the running back, whose time at Notre Dame included a prominent role on the 1966 national championship team.

His reprieve in the public speaking realm came in the early days of his 12-year pro football career with the NFL's Pittsburgh Steelers.

A nun from St. Margaret's Catholic Grade School in Pittsburgh called Steelers owner Art Rooney to inquire about having one of the Steelers speak at the school's athletic banquet. She specifically asked for quarterback Terry Bradshaw. Rooney then related to the nun that Bradshaw's minimum appearance fee was $500.

Courtesy of Notre Dame Sports Information

#28

ROCKY BLEIER

HALFBACK

PLAYING YEARS:
1965-1967

CLAIM TO FAME:
Member of Notre
Dame's 1966 national
championship squad,
but whose identity is
much more closely tied
to his post-Notre Dame
life as a Vietnam veter-
an who beat the odds
to become a fullback
on the vintage
Pittsburgh Steelers
teams of the 1970s

HIGH SCHOOL:
St. Xavier High

HOMETOWN:
Appleton, Wisconsin

PROFESSION:
Motivational speaker;
also has a cell phone
tower business

**CURRENTLY RESIDES
IN:**
Mt. Lebanon,
Pennsylvania

Courtesy of Rocky Bleier

"She says, 'Well, do you think that nice Mr. [Joe] Greene could come speak?'" Bleier related. "And Mr. Rooney says, 'Well, I think he also charges $500, but I'll ask him, sister.'

"She says, 'Oh, well do you have anybody for free?' And he says, 'Yeah, we can send Bleier.' And that's how it got going."

Eventually, Bleier began to charge too—but he'd settle for $25 here, a free meal there in those days.

"You've got to remember," he said, "I wasn't making very much money, and for a while I was on the bottom of the totem pole with the Steelers."

It didn't make the Appleton, Wisconsin, native's story any less compelling— a story that eventually became a book—*Fighting Back*—and an ABC Movie of the Week of the same title.

About the time he was graduating from Notre Dame with a degree in business management, Bleier was drafted by the Steelers in the 16th round. To illustrate what a long shot that made him, the NFL Draft these days comprises only seven rounds.

The son of a tavern owner was confronted for the first time with what life after football might look like. The picture was fuzzy, to say the least.

"Even now I don't know what I would have done had I not made the Steelers," he said. "If I didn't make the team, I was going to head down to Florida for three weeks, look up some people from school and then kind of decide what I was going to do with my life. That's how uncertain I was. Going back to Wisconsin and running the bar with my dad was an option, but not one I really wanted to even seriously consider."

During Bleier's nondescript rookie season, fate intervened. In December of 1968, he was drafted again—this time by the U.S. Army. By the following May he was in combat in Chu Lai, South Vietnam. Three months later, he was wounded in the right thigh during an ambush. He sustained further damage moments later while lying on the ground. A grenade exploded near him, sending pieces of shrapnel into his right leg and foot.

Initially he was not expected to walk again, at least not without considerable pain. Playing football was more than an absurd wish, seemingly. Bleier's only solace in the days that followed was a postcard he received from Rooney while in a hospital in Tokyo, Japan, where Bleier was recovering.

Once Bleier returned stateside, his transition back into football was laborious if not discouraging. He spent the 1970 season on the physically-unable-to-perform list and the '71 season on the taxi squad, though he was activated on several occasions.

But by the summer of 1973, he had been waived twice by coach Chuck Noll and didn't appear to be any closer to moving toward a permanent or prominent role with the team than he was before he went to Vietnam.

"To that point, the only really good thing about being on the team was that it gave me a chance to talk about my experience in Vietnam," Bleier said. "I think I needed that. I think a lot of guys from 'Nam needed that. I was fortunate, because people, the media, kind of forced me to talk about it, what it was like over there.

"A lot of other guys didn't have that opportunity, because nobody ever asked them. If you don't have anyone who wants to listen, who can empathize with you, you kind of shut down and don't talk about it—especially with Vietnam, where there was such a stigma about it. Nobody wanted to talk to those guys.

"A lot of people called them 'baby killers.' People spat on them. They couldn't even go the VFW halls, because they were run by the World War II guys. Those guys from 'Nam had to repress their feelings. I feel fortunate, because I *had* to deal with it. It became a part of my story and a part of my life."

Still, the 205-pound fullback, who came back weighing a scant 165 pounds and willed himself back into shape, wanted to walk away from it all in the summer of 1973. He had taken a job selling insurance that offseason and was miserable. A friend talked him into coming back to Steelers camp, if nothing else to make the Steelers cut him rather than making it easy on them.

Bleier not only made the team, but his career began to take off. By 1974, he was a member of the starting backfield. The pinnacle came in 1976, when he rushed for more than 1,000 yards and scored the go-ahead touchdown in Super Bowl XIII.

Bleier retired from football in 1980 and remains much more identified with his years with the Steelers than his time at Notre Dame.

"That doesn't mean Notre Dame wasn't a great experience," Bleier said. "People sometimes ask me what stands out most about my college career. It wasn't the national championship. It wasn't running out of the tunnel into the stadium. It was the coaching.

"Ara Parseghian and his staff—especially [backfield coach] Tom Pagna—were so good at coaching the little things. How to block, who to block, how to get into a left-handed stance. Without that kind of coaching, I never would have made it in the pros."

Robert Patrick Bleier—dubbed Rocky as an infant by the customers at his father's tavern—never gave much thought about coming to Notre Dame while growing up in Wisconsin.

"Even though I had gone to Catholic school, I didn't know a lot about Notre Dame," he said. "I read *Knute Rockne, All American*, because I had to do a book report on it. And I knew Notre Dame was in South Bend—wherever that was. I wasn't great in geography."

Bleier visited just three schools during the recruiting process—Wisconsin, Boston College and Notre Dame.

"Wisconsin was just too big," Bleier said. "It came down to BC and Notre Dame, and I really, really liked Boston. So I came home and did what every good Catholic boy is taught to do, and that's go to church and pray for guidance. . . . And then I did what my mother wanted me to do, and I went to Notre Dame."

Bleier's mother also gave him a piece of advice years later. Just because he had triumphed over tremendous adversity didn't mean the adversity would end. And that became part of Bleier's message.

His first marriage splintered after 17 years before ending in divorce. His first post-football job, working as a sportscaster, helped him transition into the "real world" but left him feeling unfulfilled. He tried color commentary on football broadcasts, but found himself to be colorless.

"I could do well from a script, but I couldn't ad-lib," he said. "I kind of froze up. I was stiff. I sucked, actually."

Even speaking has had its tough moments. A couple of years ago in Charlotte, while Bleier was giving a speech, someone rifled through his bag backstage and stole three of his four Super Bowl rings.

"I'll get them replaced," he said. "I learned when you get knocked down, you have to get back up. It's not just what I tell people. It's how I live."

NED BOLCAR

N ed Bolcar was coming out of church on a beautiful spring Sunday in 1994, his heart full of ambition, his mind trying to decide his next career move.

The former Notre Dame linebacker only knew that move would not involve football. His 27-year-old body had undergone a pair of surgeries on the ankles, one on each wrist, athroscopic surgery on the left knee, reconstructive surgery on the right knee and a hip injury in which the muscles and ligaments were so shredded it took seven months of intensive rehab just to be able to jog again.

Coaching was the next logical step on Bolcar's path, he figured, but his foray into that profession lasted less than a year. Spending time as an assistant high school coach in Florida fed his passion for competition, but little else. The hours were too irregular, the paychecks too small, the talent too unpredictable, the path to greatness too winding.

"In the end, I didn't want my future being determined by 16- and 17-year-old kids," he said.

The folks back in Bolcar's hometown of Phillipsburg, New Jersey, still identified him with football, though. He was the coverboy back in the early years of *USA Today*, when the national newspaper ran a diary of his recruiting experience that concluded with the prep All-America linebacker choosing Notre Dame over Penn State, Boston College, Ohio State, and Stanford.

He earned All-America honors at Notre Dame, was a rare two-time captain, shined in the classroom, stayed off the police blotter, said all the right things even when all the right things weren't happening to him.

Courtesy of Joe Raymond

Courtesy of Ned Bolcar

#47

NED BOLCAR

LINEBACKER

PLAYING YEARS:
1986-1989

CLAIM TO FAME:
Second-team All-
American in 1987 who
came back to earn
those honors again in
1989 after getting dis-
placed from the starting
lineup in 1988; as a
high school senior, did
a recruiting diary for
USA Today

HIGH SCHOOL:
Phillipsburg High

HOMETOWN:
Phillipsburg, New
Jersey

PROFESSION:
Executive vice president
of domestic sales trad-
ing for Jefferies &
Company, Inc.

**CURRENTLY RESIDES
IN:**
Warren, New Jersey

So here he was standing at his career crossroads, proud that his Notre Dame education would provide him an array of options, when an older gentleman from the congregation encroached on Bolcar's private moment of reflection.

"He said, 'Ned, I'm so sorry. I just feel terrible.'" Bolcar related. "He said, 'We thought you were going to play a long time in the NFL.'

"You would have thought I had just died."

Actually, it was a rebirth of sorts. Bolcar was about to embark on a lucrative career on Wall Street in New York. It took three months of sleeping on team-mate Wes Pritchett's brother's couch to land his first job in the business and a couple of more years to figure out where he wanted to go with it. But today he couldn't be happier with his professional life's direction.

"They call me an executive vice president of domestic sales trading for Jefferies & Company," said Bolcar, now living in Warren, New Jersey, and engaged to former Notre Dame softball standout Sheri Beth Quinn of Jupiter, Florida. "But everybody's a vice president or president or has some kind of title. I'm not a manager, though. I'm a producer."

And an avid Notre Dame football fan, too—something at one time in his life he wasn't sure would endure.

Much of that had to do with his career entangling with that of fellow All-America linebacker Michael Stonebreaker and the playing time decisions that were made along those lines. But Bolcar's Notre Dame connection was actually in peril right from the beginning of his collegiate career.

He had been so close to choosing Boston College, for the city of Boston, or Penn State, because the Nittany Lions were building toward a national championship, but he chose the Irish at the 11th hour, because he was certain the chaos of the Gerry Faust era would get overridden by Notre Dame's tradition at some point.

That certainty buckled when Bolcar took his first road trip. The Irish were to open the 1985 season at arch-rival Michigan. And Bolcar was one of seven freshmen who made the traveling squad.

"The only way I was going to play in that game was if two buses overturned," Bolcar said. "But I was so jacked to be there. I remember being as high as a kite."

Bolcar was bouncing off the walls in the Irish locker room when a senior teammate offered him a piece of advice.

"He said, 'Hey freshman. This ain't high school football. Act like you've been here before,'" Bolcar said. "I thought to myself, 'Wow, maybe this is what college football is like. Maybe it's more businesslike.' So I took it down a couple of notches and we go out on the field, and the guys look like they're going through the motion in warmups. And it's weird.

"Then Michigan comes down the tunnel. They hit that 'M Go Blue' sign as they're coming out. They're so jacked, they had snot coming out of their noses. They had blood in their eyes. These guys were off the ground. And I turned to [teammate] George Streeter and said, 'Oh boy, we're going to get the living [crap] kicked out of us.'"

When Bolcar got back to Notre Dame's campus, he called his father with the intent of transferring—immediately.

"I said, 'I've got to get out of here. I can't be a part of this. I couldn't imagine a team being so unprepared. If this was going to be the way we played football, I wanted to go to Penn State.' I play hard. I play nasty. I play intense. The intensity of this program wasn't me. There was a general feeling of being lackadaisical. I'm surprised we even won five games that year. Something had to give."

It did. Faust resigned after the 5-6 season, and Lou Holtz took over, literally and figuratively.

"Gerry was a good guy," Bolcar said. "He just wasn't successful. And it carried over into Lou's first meeting. Guys showed up late. Guys were slouching in their chairs, just like they did under Gerry.

"Lou walked in, and Chuck Lanza had his feet propped up against the stage. Lou looked down and said, 'Son, how long have you been playing football?' And Chuck said something like 13, 14 years. And Lou said, 'Well your career's coming to an end in three seconds unless you put your ass against the back of that chair and sit up.' And you heard 130 people—boom, boom, boom—everybody sat up straight. And I'm thinking, 'OK, there's a new sheriff in town.'"

Holtz went on to detail what he saw wrong with the program, chart how and when the Irish would win a national championship and warned the players to get to bed early for the next day's 6 a.m. workout.

By the time Notre Dame opened with Michigan in the fall of 1986, the whole mind-set of the team had changed, and nowhere was it more evident than in the pregame warmups that day. Notre Dame was going through its receiving drills from the 20-yard line toward the end zone when the Michigan players emerged from the Notre Dame Stadium tunnel.

Instead of running toward the sidelines, the Wolverines ran straight through Notre Dame's practice formations.

"John Kolesar was one of their stud receivers," Bolcar said. "He runs right through our line and Tom Rehder, who's 6-7 and pushing 300 and who had arms as long as my body, clotheslines Kolesar and drops him to the ground. And all hell breaks loose. Fights everywhere. And I said, 'OK, this is why I came to Notre Dame. We don't take stuff from anybody.' Lou had told us nobody was going to come into our stadium and intimidate us anymore.

"Yes, we went 5-6 that season and we lost the Michigan game [24-23], but it was a world of difference. We set the tone at that moment. The intensity and toughness were back. You could tell we were building toward something big."

Bolcar himself was Notre Dame's leading tackler the next season in 1987, with the Irish going 8-4. Stonebreaker, a talented sophomore linebacker who lettered as a freshman in '86, sat out the 1987 season due to academic difficulties.

But when Stonebreaker returned in 1988, he pushed Bolcar out of the starting lineup, even though Bolcar was a preseason Butkus Award candidate, emblematic of the nation's top linebacker, and had really done nothing to lose the spot. The Irish went on to win the national title in '88, but Bolcar couldn't move past the demotion.

"I was told I was going to rotate in, but no, I wasn't okay with it," Bolcar said. "I was friends with Mike, but I don't think I was being treated fairly. I wasn't going to speak out to the press, because I thought that would make me a bad leader, a bad captain.

"I still had a fifth year I could come back for in 1989, but I thought very seriously about not coming back for it. But it's a good thing I did. Had I left at that time, I'm convinced I would have never come back to campus again. I had a bad taste in my mouth. All I wanted to do was be treated fairly."

In the end, Bolcar's love of the school won out. The 1987 All-American returned for the 1989 season determined to beat out Stonebreaker, a 1988 All-American, if that's what it took. Fate intervened, though. Stonebreaker was injured in a car accident in the offseason, breaking a kneecap and dislocating a hip in February of 1989. The school suspended him for that season due to circumstances related to the accident.

Bolcar was again Notre Dame's leading tackler in 1989, won All-America honors and moved on to the Seattle Seahawks as a sixth-round draft choice. His first pro play was an interception of a pass thrown by Chicago Bears quarterback Jim Harbaugh.

But a series of injuries and being in the wrong places at the wrong times ravaged Bolcar's chance to extend his collegiate success into the NFL. He walked away with no regrets and a happy ending, even though perhaps not all the folks in Phillipsburg came to terms with that.

He crosses paths in the financial industry with former Fighting Irish football players of his era Wes Pritchett, Mike Brennan, and Pete Graham among others. Bolcar worked with his brother for a time at Jefferies & Company, lives 40 minutes from his mom and comes back to Notre Dame every chance he gets.

"Some of the best times in my life and the worst times in my life happened at Notre Dame, and it will always be a part of me," Bolcar said. "I wanted to play on the biggest platform in college football, and I did. I wanted to be in a peer group that appreciated education and was looking to the future, not just five years of playing football and then trying to figure out what to do with the rest of their lives. And I did that, too.

"I carry that Notre Dame experience through everything I do. When times get tough, I know I have the perseverance and the integrity to get through it."

Where Have You Gone?

REGGIE
BROOKS

R eggie Brooks no longer talks football with his older brother, Tony, never reminisces about their glory days as running backs at Notre Dame . . . or even how pro football coldly pushed each of them away.

That's not to say Reggie doesn't think about football more than intermittently anymore. In fact, coaching is something that the younger Brooks has dabbled in and wouldn't mind jumping into with both feet, someday, somehow. But with a wife, four children ranging in ages from 14 to two, and a steady job in his alma mater's technology department, reality takes precedence over dreams at this juncture of his life.

"Coaching is a pretty tough industry to crack," said Reggie, who in 1992 became the first running back to crack the 1,000-yard barrier in a season during the Lou Holtz Era after languishing through three seasons of position swaps and long stretches on the bench.

"I mean, I love working with young people. I think I have some knowledge to share. Coaching is really something I have a passion for. But I really don't have an inside track to get there, so it's not likely to happen anytime soon."

He thought he might be moving in that direction a couple of years ago, when he got hooked up with coaching internships with the Indianapolis Colts and the Berlin Thunder of NFL Europe. And in 2004, he had some preliminary discussions with then-Notre Dame head coach Tyrone Willingham about a role in the Irish football program, but Willingham was abruptly fired after a three-year run on November 30, 2004.

If Reggie gets frustrated with all the closing doors and dead ends, he doesn't stay that way for long. Not when he looks at the courageous way his older brother Tony deals with his own crushed aspirations.

Michael and Susan Bennett/Lighthouse Imaging

Courtesy of Joe Raymond

PLAYING YEARS:
1989-1992

CLAIM TO FAME:
First 1,000-yard rusher
at Notre Dame during
the Lou Holtz era
(1986-96)

HIGH SCHOOL:
Booker T. Washington
High

HOMETOWN:
Tulsa, Oklahoma

PROFESSION:
Change management
specialist for the
University of Notre
Dame's technology
department

**CURRENTLY RESIDES
IN:**
South Bend, Indiana

Tony—who arrived at Notre Dame in the fall of 1987, two years before Reggie—also works with computers, but only for short stretches each day. Two degenerative discs in Tony's back mean a life of constant and chronic pain. The joy in his life comes from spending time each day with his wife and four children (Tony has two other children, who do not live with him, from previous relationships). Tony and his family live just across the Indiana-Michigan border from Reggie in Cassopolis, Michigan.

"He's on disability now," Reggie said. "He had back surgery when he was playing with the Philadelphia Eagles, and it wound up getting infected. Things kind of snowballed from there.

"He can't stand or sit for any length of time. It's tough, because he was such an active person his whole life. He's always been a mentor for me, and he's even more so now because of the way he's dealing with this. I consider it a miracle he's even walking. It's even more amazing the way he handles the mental side of it."

Both Brooks brothers lived through plenty of adversity while at Notre Dame, though Tony's was largely self-inflicted.

As a sophomore, Tony was extremely productive during Notre Dame's national championship run in 1988, rushing for 667 yards (5.7 per carry), which was second most on the team in a loaded, rotating backfield. And he did it while playing with a stress fracture in his right foot and wearing a specially designed protective insole.

He didn't miss a game due to the injury that year, but he did sit out the USC game as a consequence of landing in Holtz's doghouse. Holtz sent both Brooks and fellow backfield mate Ricky Watters home the day before No. 1 Notre Dame's showdown with No. 2 USC in Los Angeles after the pair showed up late for a meeting.

The Irish went on to crush the second-ranked Trojans, 27-10, in that regular-season finale, then subdued West Virginia in the Fiesta Bowl to complete their national title run.

Tony's problems took another left turn the following season when he was exiled to neighboring Holy Cross Junior College. He did return for two more seasons (1990-91) before the NFL's Philadelphia Eagles drafted him in the fourth round in the spring of '92.

He managed to finish as Notre Dame's sixth all-time leading rusher (he has since been displaced to ninth), but his pro career ended after two nondescript seasons. An 11-yard kickoff return was his lone pro statistic.

Reggie arrived at Notre Dame in the fall of 1989 while his older brother was trying to work his way back to the Irish team. He came out of Booker T. Washington High School in Tulsa, Oklahoma, with a smaller body (five foot eight, 200 pounds to Tony's 6-2, 223-pound frame) and a smaller splash of recruiting hype, but his dreams of being an immediate and constant contributor were just as big.

He played only 11 minutes as a freshman, then got shifted to cornerback as a sophomore when Tony returned to the roster. Reggie made three starts and played in seven games as a corner in 1990, but yearned to move back to offense. He was afforded that opportunity in 1991, but saw just a little more than 16 minutes of action and toted the ball 18 times that season.

"I wasn't afraid of the competition," Reggie said. "In fact, the reason I came to Notre Dame was *because* of the competition, because they had Rick Watters and Tony and Lee Becton and Jerome Bettis and Rodney Culver, those kind of people. I felt like that competition would eventually make me better."

Eventually it did. Reggie's breakthrough season came during his senior year. His 1,343 yards that season stood as the third most in Irish history going into the 2005 season. His 7.6 career yards per carry broke Four Horseman Don Miller's mark of 6.8. And his 8.0 yards-per-carry average as a senior led the nation and helped Reggie finish fifth in the Heisman Trophy voting after ranking fifth on his *team* in rushing yards the previous season.

"I was pretty frustrated for most of my career," Reggie said. "In fact, there was a point in time after my sophomore year that I was seriously contemplating transferring. But my father always had taught me to finish what I had started. I finally got my chance to show what I could do, and it all worked out."

In more ways than just football.

Reggie ended up marrying his tutor, a Notre Dame student from San Antonio, Texas, who was on academic scholarship at the school.

Pro football, though, brought more frustration. This time, though, the pattern was reversed. Reggie was selected in the second round of the 1993 NFL Draft by the Washington Redskins. He was one of nine Irish picked in that draft, with four going in the first round (Rick Mirer, Jerome Bettis, Tom Carter, and Irv Smith) and two more in the second (Demetrius DuBose and Reggie Brooks).

Reggie then became the first rookie in Redskins franchise history to crack the 1,000-yard rushing mark with 1,063 yards in 1993, but then his production and playing time swooned dramatically in subsequent years (297 yards in '94, minus-two yards in 1995). Washington coach Norv Turner blamed it on injuries. Reggie claims he was healthy enough to play, and that politics prevailed.

"I really have a lot of respect for [fellow Redskins running back] Earnest Byner," Reggie said. "During my rookie year he was instrumental in helping me develop and understand the professional level. He left, though, after my rookie year. I lost my direction and things changed. They went downhill in a hurry."

Reggie finished his NFL career as a backup with Tampa Bay in 1996. His last breath as a player came with the Barcelona Dragons of NFL Europe in 1998.

"I immediately got into the IT [information technology] field after football," Reggie said. "I had a pretty good idea all along that was something I wanted to do. I enjoy working with computers, and they're pretty much in every corner of life."

Reggie worked in the field for five years in his hometown of Tulsa before landing at Notre Dame as a change management specialist. The coaching internship in Berlin was wedged in between.

"When I was playing football at Notre Dame, I couldn't wait to get out of South Bend," he said with a chuckle. "Now it feels like home. I had applied for a job here about six months before I got this one, but they said they lost my application. I'm sure glad they found it."

So is Tony, who lives just 24 miles away. The two have grown closer since their father passed away, suddenly and unexpectedly, of congestive heart failure in August of 2002.

"Tony actually is 'Raymond Anthony Junior,'" Reggie said. "Not a lot of people know that. My dad's passing caught us all so much off-guard, because he was such a strong man. He never complained. He was such a great role model for us.

"It's funny, because Tony and he used to go at it all the time, but that was because they were so much alike. And they're still alike. Tony has become such a great husband and father. He knows what's important in life. I only wish he had a chance to do all the things he wants to do."

Instead Reggie carries the dreams for both of them now.

"I'm not sure I can get this coaching bug out of my system," he said. "I tried to help out at my daughter's middle school (Brown Intermediate Center), but you have to be very careful what you say, because you don't want to hurt feelings.

"It would be great if it happens. I'll be fine if it doesn't. But I'm not giving up on it. I've got a great example and a great reason living just a few miles away why not to give up."

Where Have You Gone?

BOBBY BROWN

I f there was a real turning point in Bobby Brown's life following Notre Dame's 26-22 loss at Michigan back in the fall of 1999, it is that the swirling dreams and the burn to follow them is so much stronger and so much more defined years later.

Sure, the former Notre Dame receiver never found his way back to the NFL fringe after brief flings with the Green Bay Packers and Cleveland Browns, but that was never what Brown was about anyway.

Why else would he have graduated with three majors? Why else would he have pressed into law school instead of checking voice mail for nibbles from the Arena League or the CFL? Why else would he sit on the Notre Dame Faculty Board of Athletics, immerse himself in the South Bend community by helping out underprivileged children, and head the Black Law Students Association at Notre Dame when law school itself could easily consume all his waking hours?

"I'm an extreme visionary, so I never wanted to be considered just a football player," said Brown, who is slated to graduate from Notre Dame's law school in May of 2006 and to marry fiancée Emily Bienko three months later.

It was a two-point conversion with 4:08 left to play in Notre Dame's September 4, 1999 matchup with archrival Michigan in Ann Arbor that cloaked Brown in a hero's aura and that just as quickly dissolved.

Out of the corner of his eye, Brown spotted his brother, Terry, sitting only a few feet away in the corner of the end zone of Michigan Stadium. Bobby Brown then raised his hands to his helmet, turned his palms backward and flashed the Omega Psi Phi Fraternity sign.

A heartbeat later, a member of the officiating crew tugged at the yellow flag in his pocket and threw it in Brown's direction. The Irish were penalized 15 yards

Michael and Susan Bennett/Lighthouse Imaging

Courtesy of Joe Raymond

#88

BOBBY BROWN

WIDE RECEIVER

PLAYING YEARS:
1996-1999

CLAIM TO FAME:
Notre Dame's leading receiver in 1997 and 1999, who also gained notoriety for being penalized for flashing the Omega sign in a loss to Michigan in 1999

HIGH SCHOOL:
St. Thomas Aquinas High (Fort Lauderdale, Florida)

HOMETOWN:
Lauderhill, Florida

PROFESSION:
Student at Notre Dame Law School; also involved in real estate, freelance writing and an entertainment business

CURRENTLY RESIDES IN:
South Bend, Indiana

on the ensuing kickoff for excessive celebration. Michigan, down 22-19 after Brown's conversion catch, came back to score the winning touchdown at the 1:38 mark, thanks in part to great field position after the kickoff.

It was later reported that the official had never seen the Omega symbol before, even though athletes had been doing it for years in lieu of kneeling in prayer or hugging teammates or any number of benign forms of self-expression.

"He thought I was mimicking the Michigan fans," Brown said. "I found out later he said he made a bad call. If he knew what I was trying to do, he wouldn't have made the call.

"The true definition of ignorance is simply people not knowing. So I can't hold people accountable for not knowing. It just goes to show how far we need to go still in breaking down barriers between black and white America. If this incident helped, then we made progress."

Progress came slowly for Brown on a personal level. He was taunted in opposing stadiums for the rest of the season. Even some fans at Notre Dame Stadium mocked the Omega sign when Brown scored a touchdown. And he was almost flagged the next week at Purdue, instead receiving a stern warning, for pointing skyward to the Lord after a big catch.

Perhaps the most stinging reaction for Brown came from his own head coach. Even three days after the fact, Irish coach Bob Davie's scorn was terse and biting.

"By the letter of the rule, he did something he should not do," Davie said, "and Bobby Brown will have to live with it for the rest of his life."

And Brown does live with it. But he also lives with the distinction of being Notre Dame's leading receiver that ('99) season and in 1997, too. And he lives with the knowledge that he never had a toxic attitude or lost the respect of his teammates during a down statistical year in 1998—a season in which he played with but never publicly acknowledged a serious wrist injury.

"No matter if it was a good year or a bad year, a good play or a bad play, my teammates know I was going to play with the same tenacity," Brown said. "People knew I didn't take any mess from anyone. And the year I didn't have many catches [1998], I was the best blocker on the team. It's something I took a lot of pride in.

"Still [1998] was a humbling experience, because I wanted to catch the ball, but it was also taste of life. Sometimes you've got to take a role that gets a lot less notoriety, but it's how you approach your goal and your commitment to the team—or company or family—that determines what kind of person you are and what kind of character you'll have throughout your life."

It was Brown's mother, Bettye, and his brother, Terry, who helped shape his character in his formative years in Lauderhill, Florida, and still do today.

There were still plenty of opportunities to succumb to ills and problems prevalent in his South Florida neighborhood. His own father, Willie Brown, had done so and spent most of Brown's childhood locked up in a correctional facility.

"There are obviously some negatives with that," said Bobby, born Braynard O. Brown and the youngest of five children in his family. "But there were also some positives. My mother was an educator who worked very hard. But I saw her work even harder as a single parent, taking on extra jobs so she could purchase a vehicle and so she could put my brother through Columbia University. And she did it in a time, the 1980s, when women—black women—were not afforded a lot of the opportunities that were afforded to other people.

"I was 12 years old when I made up my mind I was going to be a lawyer. I was 12 years old when I made up my mind that I was going to put myself in position to get a full scholarship, both athletically and academically. Those are all byproducts of watching what my mother went through. While it was rough, it was exactly what I needed, and it built within me a character that I don't see failure as an option. I just feel as though when I see a door that's closed, it's just a matter to time before I can knock it down. She's not only my mom. She's my hero."

It was Terry Brown, Bobby's other hero, who gave his little brother the conviction to speak his mind.

Terry played football at Columbia University, then went to law school and is now a federal prosecutor in Fort Lauderdale, Florida, and head of his own narcotics division. He is also a youth minister at his church, a peewee football coach and the president of the National Black Prosecutors Association.

"He extends himself so much further than just the legal community," Bobby said. "And that's what I'm trying to do now. It makes life hectic, but I'd rather be busy than bored. And when I graduate, I definitely want to be a community leader in a lot of different fashions. I don't ever want to put myself in a box."

He doesn't even come close. In addition to his aforementioned activities, he also dabbles in real estate and writes a sports column for *Irish Sports Report*. The place where he feels like he has made the greatest impact, however, is on the Notre Dame Faculty Board, where he serves as the student representative. Recently retired Notre Dame president the Rev. Edward A. Malloy appointed Brown to the board in 2003.

"The board is made up mostly of older white men," Brown said. "I'm the only African-American on the board, so it gives me an opportunity to be a unique voice. Obviously we don't always agree, but the manner in which we disagree and express those disagreements is very positive and is something I hope is a microcosm of society, because America is still an older white man's society. We still have an uphill battle for true diversity. Down the road, I hope to do something about that on a broader scale—in my community, and in the nation, to be honest.

"I don't want to be someone coming from a biased standpoint. I want to be open-minded, but I also want to take full advantage of the opportunity to share, as an African-American and as a former football player, the things I think need to be heard."

Brown used to talk to his first college coach, Lou Holtz, about those types of things. The two grew so close that Brown still refers to Holtz as "my white father." But after Brown redshirted under Holtz in 1995 and played for him as a reserve in 1996, Holtz resigned and was replaced by Davie.

"Lou Holtz *is* the reason I came to Notre Dame," Brown said. "He sat in my mother's living room and promised my mother he was going to be more than a coach to me, and he kept every one of his promises. That's why it was so hard when he left. My whole recruiting class, we held meetings in the dorm and we were all going to transfer, but Coach Holtz encouraged us not to do that. But that shows you what kind of guy he is. He's still like a father to me."

Brown's own father is out of prison now. His parents have separated, but Bettye still invites Willie Brown over for holidays when Bobby is in town.

"I wouldn't say he's a big part of my life," Brown said. "But I do love him. My mother taught me that. I definitely do not like some of his ways, some of the choices he's made in his life, but I love him and I know he loves me, despite some of the mistakes he's made."

And those are the kind of emotions Bobby Brown was carrying around that day at Michigan. All the angst, all the tribulations, all the heartache that he was in the process of overcoming. And then he spots brother Terry, a beacon in all the chaos past and present.

"I didn't have a lot of positive male role models in my life," Brown said. "But I chose to follow one who [was]. He's a big reason I made the sign that day. And I'm proud I did it. He's a great role model for anyone."

And now, so too is Bobby Brown.

Where Have You Gone?

DEREK BROWN

D erek Brown always told himself that he didn't want football to define him—at least from the ninth grade on, when Brown's mother finally relented and let him play the sport for the first time.

He had a college degree from Notre Dame, a dynamic personality, some name recognition from almost a decade in the NFL and a healthy bank account. But for the first time in his life, the former Notre Dame standout tight end and NFL first-round draft choice felt lost.

"That lost feeling, it only got worse," said Brown as he was trying to transition into life after football in 2000 and beyond. "You always tell yourself you're going to be ready when football ends. I always pictured myself as a businessman, but you're really not prepared for that, no matter how much you think or hope that you are.

"You're going from a very structured lifestyle to an unstructured one. It's almost like coming out of the military. And professional sports adds another layer to it, because almost never do you get to leave on your own terms. You either get hurt or you get cut. Even a guy like John Elway. Sure, he might have won two Super Bowls, but I guarantee you he can barely walk. He feels it. Every day something is aching on him."

For Brown what was aching was his ego mostly, at least at first. His last roster spot came with the Arizona Cardinals in 2000. His last catch was two years prior in Oakland. His only touchdown in nine pro seasons came in 1997 with Jacksonville. The last time the term "upside" was used to describe his career was during his three seasons with the New York Giants (1992-94), the team that drafted him with the 14th pick overall.

"I don't think I lived up to my full potential at all," Brown said. "I felt I could have contributed much more if a) I had more opportunity or b) learned quick-

#86

DEREK BROWN

TIGHT END

PLAYING YEARS:
1988-1991

CLAIM TO FAME:
Burst onto the scene as a freshman and became a key figure in Notre Dame's national title run in 1988; went on to earn All-America honors as a senior in 1991

HIGH SCHOOL:
Merritt Island High

HOMETOWN:
Merritt Island, Florida

PROFESSION:
Owns three Quiznos Sub shops in the Northeast

CURRENTLY RESIDES IN:
Clifton Park, New York

© Cheryl A. Ertelt

Courtesy of Derek Brown

er. Up until that point, the game came easy to me. But I have no regrets other than that it ended too soon. I was a salary cap casualty. It wasn't that I couldn't play anymore. I was too expensive. But I did get to play the greatest team sport in the world for nine years professionally, which is great.

"Where that leaves you, though, is that you still need a job. Well, I had been trying to figure out for some time what I was going to do when I grew up. The only problem was I wasn't sure I was actually going to grow up, but I still needed something to do. Some of it's a financial thing after you leave football, but a lot of it is having a purpose in your life. I've always been a big dreamer anyway."

Brown's vocation these days isn't exactly a dream or a passion but something he learned to love—after he stopped trembling. He owns three Quiznos sub shops in the Northeast part of the country, with the hopes of eventually expanding that number to 20 to 30.

"We can joke about it now," said Brown, who went into business with childhood friend Suresh Rajan. "We always told each other, 'There's nothing to this. It's just a matter of putting your [cards] on the table. We're those kind of guys. We can take risks.' But let me tell you, until you stroke that first big check, it's like jumping off a cliff."

Brown and Rajan—a USC grad and a rabid Miami Hurricanes fan incidentally—opened their first store June 30, 2004, in Pittsfield, Massachusetts. Store No. 2 followed roughly three months later and store No. 3 became a reality in March of 2005.

"Quiznos is a very, very good brand," Brown said. "And it's new here in the Northeast, so there's plenty of room to grow."

What brought Brown to the Northeast—specifically Clifton Park, New York, just north of Albany—was his wife Kristin, and to a lesser extent his mother-in-law.

The Browns were living in the Phoenix area after Derek had been cut by the Cardinals. He continued to work out, though, in the hopes that this trip to the waiver wire wouldn't be permanent. In the meantime, Kristin's sister, 31 years old at the time, developed breast cancer.

"Kristin wanted to go back to upstate New York, which was home, to help her sister through this," said Brown, who has two kids, both under the age of seven. "I tried to go back and forth, but after a while I saw I wasn't going to get picked up by another team. So I figured why not move back East for good. Now my dream would have been to live in Laguna Niguel, California, but my mother-in-law wasn't going to have any of that—not with two grandchildren. It's turned out to be a great move all the way around. And the best part of it is, Kristin's sister went through all the chemo and the treatments and is doing great now."

Brown's path to Notre Dame was a little more capricious. Brown's father was an IBM systems analyst when Derek was growing up, and the elder Brown's job had taken the family to five different states by the time Derek was eight. Finally, they settled in Merritt Island, Florida, near the Kennedy Space Center.

It wasn't until Brown was pushing six foot six that his mom became convinced that *he* wasn't the one who was running the risk of getting hurt on the football field. Brown was a ninth-grader by then, and it didn't take long for people to frame him as a college prospect.

"By the time I was a junior, I was convinced I was going to the University of Florida," Brown said. "I dreamed about myself as a Florida Gator. There was no way I wasn't going to be a Florida Gator, and no one could talk me out of it, but then people started telling me I *should* be a Florida Gator. And that turned me off. Well, nobody was going to tell me what to do."

His choices then came down to Notre Dame and Miami. He hadn't even really followed Notre Dame football up to that point, didn't know much about the tradition, either.

"It literally came down to a gut feeling," he said. "I was home by myself and I popped in the tape, 'Wake Up The Echoes.' I got goose bumps on the back of my neck. That was it—I had to go. Of course the hard part was telling [then-Miami coach] Jimmy Johnson 'no' twice in my family room. I asked my dad if he could do it for me, but he said, 'No son, this is one of those things you have to do in life.' I'm glad I had the strength to do it."

Brown also had the strength to make an impact early in his All-America career at Notre Dame. He scored touchdowns on his first two collegiate receptions, broke into the starting lineup by the middle of his freshman season (1988) and went on to start 37 straight games to finish his career.

The Irish won the national title during Brown's freshman year and went 43-7 during his four years under coach Lou Holtz. He closed his career, fittingly, against the University of Florida. The 18th-ranked Irish upended the No. 3 Gators, 39-28, in the Sugar Bowl, January 1, 1992 in New Orleans.

"Playing for Lou Holtz was great," Brown said. "What made it even better was that a lot of the lessons I learned in football from Lou, I was able to apply to the business world—like asking yourself, 'What's important now?' setting goals and taking care of the little things."

In Brown's rookie year with the Giants (1992), he came across a coach who reminded him a lot of Holtz—not in stature or demeanor, but in many other ways. He was New York's running backs coach at the time. Today Charlie Weis is Notre Dame's head football coach.

"I just thought he was an excellent coach back then," Brown said. "He was very organized, very focused. He also knew there was more to you than just being a player. That made me like him as a person. I think he's going to do excellent things for Notre Dame. I think he was an excellent selection. If I were picking colleges all over again, he's a guy I'd love to play for."

IVORY COVINGTON

H e has settled inconspicuously into the nine-to-five life, though often it's more like nine-to-seven or six-to-six.

Ivory Covington still packs a modest 165 pounds on his five-foot-10 frame eight years after he played his last competitive football game. He talks the corporate talk, walks the corporate walk, but he dreams well beyond the confines of his cubicle at Deloitte Consulting.

Those dreams, incidentally, have nothing to do with football.

"I'm an IT [information technology] consultant, and I've been one since I graduated," said Covington, a former cornerback at Notre Dame in the mid '90s, living single in Atlanta. "I enjoy the IT field. I'm pretty good at it. It pays well and there are plenty of perks, but I've come to realize it's not my passion. Real estate is."

It's been building toward that over the past three years. Covington has combed through real estate books, gone to seminars, even puttered around with some investments.

"I'm in the process of creating my own company," he said. "Actually, the name has already been filed. It's called *The Ivory Company*, and it will be a real estate investment and development firm. I'm pretty excited and determined to make it work."

Which, as history suggests, is bad news for anyone getting in Covington's way. Just ask Ron Leshinski, a six-foot-two, 240-pound tight end when he played for the U.S. Military Academy back in the mid-'90s.

The two haven't crossed paths since their fateful meeting on the football field a decade ago, but they've traded sentiments through chance meetings of friends.

Courtesy of Notre Dame Sports Information

Courtesy of The Ivory Company, LLC

PLAYING YEARS:
1994-1997

CLAIM TO FAME:
Diminutive cornerback who stuffed six-foot-two, 240-pound tight end Ron Leshinski of Army at the one-foot line on a two-point conversion attempt to preserve Notre Dame's 28-27 victory over Army in 1995

HIGH SCHOOL:
Dunwoody High

HOMETOWN:
Decatur, Georgia

PROFESSION:
IT consultant for Deloitte Consulting

CURRENTLY RESIDES IN:
Atlanta, Georgia

"It is my understanding he still can't believe what happened," Covington said of Leshinski, "but he has been a good sport about it."

It was supposed to be a soft spot in the 1995 Notre Dame football schedule, a meeting with heavy underdog Army in mid-October at Giants Stadium in East Rutherford, New Jersey.

The Irish had just come out of a stretch in which they played No. 13 Texas, No. 7 Ohio State and No. 15 Washington in consecutive weeks—winning two of three—with fifth-ranked USC to follow the Army clash.

But the Cadets rolled up a stunning 365 yards rushing that day and took advantage of some sloppiness on the part of the Irish offense to rally to within 28-27 with 39 seconds left in the game. Army scored its final touchdown on a rare pass, a seven-yarder from Ronnie McAda to Leon Gantt, and looked to catch the Irish off guard with another toss on the two-point conversion try.

This time on the receiving end it was Leshinski, who would go on to dabble in pro football while finishing up his military commitment in the National Guard and who even played on the 1999 World Bowl champion Frankfurt Galaxy team.

When Leshinski caught the ball against the Irish, all that stood between him and a seismic upset of the 17th-ranked Irish was Notre Dame's lithe sophomore cornerback. Covington, though, proceeded to tattoo Leshinski into the Giants Stadium turf one foot shy of the goal line. Notre Dame rode the momentum of that stick to a 38-10 conquest of fifth-ranked USC the next week, then three more wins to secure a berth in the Orange Bowl opposite Florida State.

"In football you just kind of react instinctively," Covington said of the play. "I definitely remember thinking that it was crunch time and we had to do something to stop this team. I just happened to be in the right position.

"To tell you the truth, it didn't feel much different than any other tackle until my teammates started jumping on me. I mean I didn't think, 'Oh my goodness, this guy's almost twice my size.' It was more like, 'He has the ball. He has to go down—no ifs, ands or buts about it.' I've been that way since I started playing football. I never saw a tackle I wanted to turn down."

Covington's career statistics at Notre Dame bear that out. He finished with 156 tackles for the Irish, and 122 of those were solos.

Among the mementos that came Covington's way from that Army game was a package he received a few days later from television personality and Notre Dame graduate Regis Philbin.

In it were articles clipped from the New York papers as well as a congratulatory letter. Covington and Philbin would meet later in person at a Notre Dame pep rally.

"It's funny I was in New York [in the spring of 2005], and I decided to take in his TV show [*Live with Regis and Kelly*]," Covington said. "I was just going to sit in the audience and watch, but I started talking with some of his people that it would be great to talk to him.

"They passed along the message and the next thing I know I'm up in his office reliving the play all over again. To Regis, it was like it was just yesterday. He remembered everything about the game, remembered sending me the articles. It was great."

Perhaps the reason the diminutive cornerback approached the game with a linebacker's mentality is that he was one for most of his football career growing up. His growth spurt came and went early while he was excelling at sports and in the classroom in Los Angeles.

By the time his mother, Beverly, took a job transfer to Atlanta after Covington's freshman year in high school, though, he no longer looked linebacker-sized compared to the other kids and was moved to the secondary at Dunwoody (Georgia) High School.

Maybe it was destiny or simply something in the water that would help the new free safety find stardom there. In Covington's junior year, the strong safety he played alongside was a senior named Ryan Seacrest.

Seacrest has gone on to garner a star on the Hollywood Walk of Fame from his work in radio and his role as host on the TV series *American Idol*. Seacrest was replaced in the Dunwoody lineup at strong safety the next season by a kid by the name of Kip Pardue.

Pardue went on to play football at Yale, then got into modeling and acting in Hollywood. His breakthrough film was *Remember The Titans*, in which he played the hippie California quarterback Ronnie "Sunshine" Bass.

Even Covington's coach at Dunwoody, who guided the school to a 15-0 record and a state title Covington's senior season, has gained a measure of notoriety.

David Kelly later became a college assistant coach and was a member of George O'Leary's staff at Georgia Tech when O'Leary landed the Notre Dame head coaching job in December of 2001. Kelly, in fact, was one of three assistants O'Leary took with him to Notre Dame, but O'Leary's stint at the school lasted less than a week when inaccuracies were discovered in his biographical information.

It was too late for Kelly to do a U-turn back to Georgia Tech when O'Leary resigned, so he landed instead at Stanford as an assistant several weeks later, after Cardinal head coach Tyrone Willingham took the Notre Dame job. Kelly has since moved on to Duke as its offensive coordinator.

"Coach Kelly was a lot like Coach [Lou] Holtz," Covington said. "Both of them have had a huge impact on me. They both wanted to prepare you for football and life after it. They both wanted to develop the whole person."

Covington most definitely took that message to heart. When his college football eligibility expired after the 1997 season, he didn't entertain a single thought about attending an NFL tryout camp, preferring instead to sift through a stack of job offers in the business world.

"It was a conscious decision on my part," Covington said. "It wasn't that I didn't think I couldn't play in the NFL. I didn't want to. I had a lot of people question my decision, because it didn't make sense to them. I still loved the game. I'm a huge Notre Dame fan, but it was time to take it off the front burner. I have no regrets, and I've never looked back."

Covington, in fact, looks forward—literally. He is a teacher/mentor in Atlanta's Junior Achievement Program, working with fourth-graders.

"I had a lot of mentors growing up, who really helped me achieve," he said. "I just wanted to give something back."

Those fourth-graders weren't even born when Covington moved into the national spotlight for the first time with the tackle of Leshinski, but somehow the word of the tackle gets out. It does at Covington's workplace too, and just about everywhere he travels.

"I don't know how people find out about," he said with a laugh. "I don't see what relevance it has now. I don't even bring up football, but somehow it comes up all the time in conversation. It's not the thing I remember when I look back at Notre Dame. The friendships fill my memories. But that tackle? I was just doing my job."

Where Have You Gone?

BOB CRABLE

T he whir becomes a rumble as the Harley approaches the parking lot at Moeller High School in Cincinnati.

Occasionally the rider shows up without a helmet. Never does Bob Crable, though, arrive without a smile.

"My wife just let me get it," said Crable, a former All-America linebacker at Notre Dame. "I wanted a motorcycle ever since I got married. Well sometime after I turned 40, I was looking at one and I said, 'Wouldn't that be great?' And she turned to me and said, 'You can have it.' Well it didn't take me long to make the purchase."

But it did come with one stipulation.

"If I let any of our kids near it, she'll castrate me," Crable said with a laugh.

At Moeller, the Harley raised a few eyebrows initially, considering Crable is a religion teacher at the school and Moeller's head football coach. Then again, Crable has always blazed his own trail in his own way, including in his coaching.

Especially in his coaching.

Gerry Faust was Crable's own head football coach throughout his high school career at Moeller and also his college coach in Crable's final season at Notre Dame (1981). Faust's failures at Notre Dame may have sent his own coaching career into oblivion, but his success at Moeller was so prolific that when he was hired at Notre Dame after the 1980 season, people may have asked "why?" but rarely did they ask "who?" During Crable's four years under Faust at Moeller, the Crusaders didn't lose a game.

In Crable's first four years as the school's head coach, Moeller has dropped 16 games, compared with 30 wins. A 10-3 season in 2004, truncated by a loss

#43

BOB CRABLE

LINEBACKER

PLAYING YEARS:
1978-1981

CLAIM TO FAME:
Two-time All-American who holds the Notre Dame school record for tackles in a game, season and career

HIGH SCHOOL:
Archbishop Moeller High

HOMETOWN:
Cincinnati, Ohio

PROFESSION:
Religion teacher and head football coach at Cincinnati Moeller High

CURRENTLY RESIDES IN:
Miami Trails, Ohio

to eventual Division I state champ Cincinnati Colerain in the regional finals, though, has stirred memories of the Faust Era for many, including Faust himself.

But not for Crable.

"Gerry has always been a big part of my life," Crable said. "When I took the job, there were certain aspects that I wanted to bring back and that I believe in, but there are certain things that are really never going to come back.

"The school has become a more well-rounded school, but it is still known around the country for being a great football team. Gerry did a great job of putting Moeller on the map for football. The one thing I would like to accent that he taught me is when you play together and when you develop a family atmosphere, you can beat great football teams, even if they're better than you are.

"Gerry told me, 'Crabes, in 15-20 years, you're going to have as many wins as I did. Yada, yada, yada.' I said, 'Number 1, Coach, I don't want to be Gerry Faust II. I want to be Bob Crable.' People don't know how much he sacrificed in order do to what he did at Moeller High School. He'd be in at seven in the morning and leave at eight at night. Every night. He didn't get a chance to coach his kids in Little League. He didn't get a chance to do some of the things with his family that I know he would liked to have done. I have four kids myself, and I guess I'm a little bit more selfish than he is. Moeller High School is important, but I also think the good Lord put these kids in my life to teach me a little balance as well."

Crable's oldest child, Amy, recently graduated from Xavier University and got married in the spring of 2005. His youngest, Matthew, entered the third grade in the fall of 2005. Daughter Allison is a student at Moeller, becoming a sophomore in the fall of 2005. His oldest son Brian, an offensive lineman on the Moeller team, graduated from high school in the spring of '05 and is attending Butler University.

Bob Crable himself wasn't nearly as clear about his college pecking order coming out of Moeller in 1978. The consensus prep All-American, in fact, didn't make his final decision until after national signing day. And he was on the verge of signing with Michigan after visiting Ohio State, Cincinnati and Colorado.

"My visit to Notre Dame had been canceled because of a blizzard," Crable recalled. "When I did get up there, there were only about five guys there at the time and about four feet of snow on the ground. I have no idea, other than the people, why I would have picked Notre Dame at the time. My father really wanted me to go to Michigan. My mom kind of balanced the scales a bit for me and told me if it made me feel better, she'd like me to go to Notre Dame."

By the end of Crable's freshman season, though, he wanted to leave. It would have fit in well with some other sharp turns that would occur later in his life, but it didn't match his penchant to persevere.

Crable stayed and put up monster numbers at Notre Dame the next season. His 187 tackles as a sophomore in 1979 still stands as a school single-season record. In fact, no one has amassed more than 147 since. His 26 tackles against Clemson that same season still is tied for the NCAA single-game mark, while his 521 career tackles remains atop the Notre Dame all-time list.

"The game is different now," Crable said of his records. "It's much more of a passing game. You're more likely to see a 10- or 15-sack game by an individual than a 26-tackle game. It's just not the same game."

Nor was it the same when Dan Devine retired after Crable's junior year. Initially, though, Crable was thrilled when Faust was named Devine's successor.

"People were so excited, it's like we were running around on adrenaline for a while," Crable said. "Then we open with a big win against LSU and Michigan loses. We move up from Number 4 to the Number 1 spot in the country. But then reality set in."

Michigan's 25-7 ambush the next week sent Notre Dame tumbling a dozen spots to No. 13. A last-second 15-14 loss to Purdue the following week bumped the Irish from the rankings for good. The Irish finished 5-6 that season—Faust's first and Crable's last at Notre Dame. Faust would go on to a 30-26-1 mark in five seasons in South Bend, recording nine more losses than he did in 18 years at Moeller (174-17-2). He followed that with a nine-year mark of 45-53-3 at Akron.

"Coach Devine, God rest his soul, had some idiosyncrasies," Crable said. "What I learned from him was that his expertise came from the assistant coaches he assembled. They knew how to get people into the right positions. Gerry was canned emotion. One of the things I have learned as a coach, I think, is that it's not just about emotion. It's about preparation and confidence and believing in players and coaches. When you can be emotional with all that, that's pretty good stuff.

"In high school, we had some pretty good people. If we played with emotion, we could beat the dog snot out of people. In high school, Gerry called plays sometimes that weren't good plays, but our personnel was good enough to make them good plays. When you go up against Michigan, you better put yourself and your players in position to be successful. Whether Gerry did or did not, I guess history tells you that."

Crable's own history includes a seven-year run in pro football with the New York Jets that ended when both of his knees gave out. After the first injury and reconstructive surgery in 1984, Crable started his own sportswear business. He ended up selling the business after several years but stayed on and worked for the new owners.

Eventually, though, he began to question his station in life, especially when the wife of his close cousin and mentor, Jack Crable, died of breast cancer at the age of 38.

"Eventually, I blamed the corporate environment," Crable said. "I think I was in rebellion to a certain extent. If I had to do it all over again, I don't think I would have left so quickly, but I'm in the right place right now, doing the right thing, I believe."

Crable had to go back to school to get his teaching certificate in religion. And it took him several years to work himself up Moeller's coaching ladder. But the view from the top is very similar to Crable as it was on the way up, which is how Crable likes it.

"It's been a roller coaster," he said of his post-Notre Dame existence. "You look and you try to figure out what the right things to do are, whether it's selling sweatshirts or teaching kids class. I discovered there's adversity in everything you're going to do. It's just a matter of how you're going to deal with that adversity."

Where Have You Gone?

GREG DAVIS

I nvariably, the subject would come up in casual conversation, even more than a decade later. Sometimes innocently. Sometimes not.

"In all my years in the banking industry and in sales, inevitably it seemed to come up at some point," said Greg Davis, a former Notre Dame safety during the Lou Holtz era. "People would talk about your background, find out you played football at Notre Dame, and the next thing you know, they're talking about 'the clip' on Rocket Ismail's punt return. Now they didn't always put two and two together and figure out that the guy who was flagged for the clip was me, but I would let them know. I wasn't going to run away from it."

Nor did Davis do so in the weeks and months that followed "the clip."

It was January 1, 1991, and No. 1 Colorado was leading fifth-ranked Notre Dame, 10-9, in the closing moments of the Orange Bowl game in Miami, Florida. The Irish had been uncharacteristically sloppy on offense that evening, committing five turnovers and finishing the night with a modest 264 yards in total offense.

Still, the Notre Dame defense was able to push the Buffaloes backward on three consecutive plays, bringing up fourth-and-long from the Colorado 47-yard line with 43 seconds left. Instead of punting the ball out of bounds deep in Notre Dame territory, though, Buffaloes punter Tom Rouen kicked to one of the most dangerous return men in college football—Ismail.

Ismail fielded the ball on the 9, weaved through traffic and found a seam down the right sideline for what appeared to be a game-winning 91-yard punt return.

"Basically, I was sort of running with my guy downfield, and he kind of over-ran the play," Davis recalled. "At that point, I kind of turned around and saw

#26

GREG DAVIS

STRONG SAFETY

PLAYING YEARS:
1988-1991

CLAIM TO FAME:
Came back from being flagged for "the clip" on Rocket Ismail's punt return in the 1991 Orange Bowl loss to Colorado and played through injuries to become a solid contributor in the fall of 1991

HIGH SCHOOL:
McArthur High

HOMETOWN:
Hollywood, Florida

PROFESSION:
Stock market investor

CURRENTLY RESIDES IN:
Charlotte,
North Carolina

Rocket stumbling, and I saw a guy sort of closing in on him. I just dived, trying to get my body between him and Rocket. I thought I caught him on the side. But as I was laying on the ground, I saw the ref throwing the flag. Later, when I looked at film, it really looked like it could have gone either way. I just wish he had thrown the flag earlier rather than waiting until Rocket had broken into the clear."

Holtz and most of Davis's bewildered teammates didn't even know who had been flagged for the clip until Davis stepped forward on the sideline and volunteered that it was him.

Adding to the heartache for Davis that night was that this was one of the few games in his college career that his family got to see him play in person. He had grown up less than 20 miles away in Hollywood, Florida, a perfect scenario for a Hollywood ending.

As far as Davis's mom, Irene, is concerned, she did get that storybook finish. It just took a while longer to unravel. Fourth months after the Orange Bowl, she saw her youngest child get a Notre Dame degree—in person. Then the next fall she watched him from afar—not only returning for a fifth year, but courageously fighting through a separated shoulder, a torn knee ligament and a position change to outside linebacker.

Irene Davis then saw him push forward into the real world when pro football dangled only flimsy paths to prolong that passion. Ultimately, she saw him mature into a loving husband and father, her ultimate dream. Davis currently lives in Charlotte, North Carolina, with his wife, Suelan, and infant daughter Ryann Nicole.

"I got out of banking and into individual investing about three and a half years ago," Davis said. "I get to set my own hours and work from home. That means I get to be there for my daughter's first words, first steps, a lot of things other fathers miss."

Davis's parents didn't have that luxury. His father worked long hours in construction, and his mom the same as a maid to support and nurture the dreams of their seven children.

"It was definitely humble beginnings," said Davis, the youngest of the kids. "There wasn't always a lot of money to go around, but there was always plenty of love. I learned to appreciate the little things. Even when I was a little kid, I realized she was giving up a lot for us. Now than I'm an adult, I realize she gave up *everything* for us to have a chance at a bright future."

Davis's future began to collide with the present at McArthur High School in Hollywood, Florida. He was a standout in the classroom and was an underrated running back and free safety in football. Still, plenty of the national football powers were able to find him. Ultimately he chose Notre Dame over Miami and Florida State.

"I liked the reputation of the school," Davis said of Notre Dame. "Plus, I really wanted to get out of the state of Florida. Now for a while, I thought maybe I got too far away. I didn't realize how cold it was in South Bend. When I was up there on my recruiting visit, I didn't notice it. I think it was because we were in and out a lot, and I was so excited to see snow for the first time. Once I got on campus in the fall, though, it seemed like we had about three warm days and then it got cold. I said, 'OK, you've just got to get out of bed and deal with this every day.' And that's what I did."

He also dealt with a slow climb up the depth chart. Initially, it was thought that Davis might stick at running back, but by spring of his freshman year, it was clear his star was rising on defense.

"I didn't care where I played," Davis said. "I just wanted to play where I could get on the field fastest, although it took me a while to get there. But I got there."

His best season, ironically, was the 1990 campaign that ended with the fateful play in the Orange Bowl. He was second on the team in tackles with 58, and no Irish defensive player logged more minutes (275).

The play didn't end, though, that night for Davis. The next day, newspapers from all over the country called Davis, asking him to relive and recount the painful memory over again. Then Davis went home for a break to South Florida, and all everyone outside of his immediate family seemed to want to talk about was the clip.

"Once that gets over with, I go back to school and everybody in the dorms asks you about it," Davis said. "It kind of goes on and on until the next season started. Finally, we had something else to look forward to. But you know, a lot of good came out of that. Coach Holtz was always supportive about it, and my teammates were great. Not once did they point a finger at me. I learned a lot about what great guys they were and what Notre Dame was all about."

He also learned a lot about himself. Davis didn't let that moment define him—not because he chose to ignore it, but because he chose to transcend it.

"My dad died last year," Davis said, "and it was very tough on all of us, especially my mom. But the one thing I'll take with me was how proud he was of me. So is my mom. And that means the world to me."

In time, football may move back into the picture for Davis. Someday he hopes to coach on the side—not as a profession, but just to give back.

"I'd like to get back to playing tennis once in a while, too, and I hope to run a marathon one day," Davis said. "But right now my daughter needs all my attention. My parents gave me a great gift—knowing what's important in my life. And no one needs to remind me what that is."

PETE DURANKO

O nly in the quietest moments does Pete Duranko stop thinking about tor-
turing his friends with his singing or his warped jokes and start asking
himself the tough questions.

Only then does the former Notre Dame All-America defensive lineman feel
the weight of a life that has segued from two years of joblessness to a battle with
a debilitating and incurable disease to a risky heart condition that required surgery in January of 2005 and that almost killed him.

Only then do the staggering statistics associated with the progressive neuro-
muscular disease called Amyotrophic Lateral Sclerosis (ALS), also known as Lou
Gehrig's Disease, look so daunting. Like the one that says the average life
expectancy after diagnosis is two to five years.

"I try to have a sense of humor, I try to be strong," said Duranko, diagnosed
with ALS in the spring of 2001. "It isn't always easy. Many times you cry. I'm
pissed off a lot of times when I think about it and I'm by myself. But those are
also the times I can make sense of it all. I'm a very religious guy. The Blessed
Mother, I think, did this for me to go out and help people to understand how
to deal with adversity."

Duranko does that by showing that teardrops are as much a part of the
process as courage, and that having a sense of humor, how ever twisted, is the
most powerful emotional salve.

"All my friends are so happy that I can't talk right now," whispered Duranko,
whose left vocal chord was paralyzed during the heart operation, temporarily
taking away the resonance in his voice. "I think I'm doing wonderfully, except I
can't sing the [Notre Dame] fight song in Polish."

Courtesy of Pete Duranko

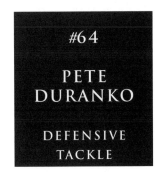

#64

PETE DURANKO

DEFENSIVE TACKLE

PLAYING YEARS:
1963-1966

CLAIM TO FAME:
Converted from a back-up fullback to become an All-America defensive lineman

HIGH SCHOOL:
Bishop McCort High School

HOMETOWN:
Johnstown, Pennsylvania

PROFESSION:
Retired and on disability; does public speaking on a volunteer basis to raise money for and awareness about ALS (Lou Gehrig's Disease)

CURRENTLY RESIDES IN:
Johnstown, Pennsylvania

Courtesy of Santiago Flores

Duranko can no longer button his own shirt anymore either, or wash himself due to the ALS. He can't get out of bed in the morning without stretching for three hours. He recently had to give up driving. He can't walk without the assistance of a walker on rollers. Yet his biggest concern is how his wife is doing with all this.

What he can and does do is offer hope. Whenever a newly diagnosed ALS victim reaches out, Duranko is the voice on the other end of the phone. When the research movement for the disease needs a human face to help raise money or awareness, Duranko gives them that—and more.

He gives it a heart, and occasionally an unsolicited singing voice.

"I was in New York [in 2004] to accept an award," he said. "And there were all these Broadway singers there people had paid to come see. So in the middle of my speech, I sang four bars of 'Some Enchanted Evening.' You know, I do sing fairly well, I think."

> *Some enchanted evening*
> *You may see a stranger*
> *You may see a stranger*
> *Across a crowded room*

Duranko, living back in his hometown of Johnstown, Pennsylvania, is no stranger to anyone afflicted with ALS. He travels to wherever money needs to be solicited or people need to be informed. He answers every e-mail, every letter, every phone call, day or night.

"People who have the disease don't know what to do, and it's scary for them," Duranko said. "The first thing I tell them is to enjoy each day. Take it one at a time. The longer you live, the more you appreciate life. That's the most important thing.

"I don't have all the answers, but I know if you work hard enough, things will work out. You won't win the Super Bowl, but you can win a couple of games here and there."

The ALS Association tells us that no two people have the same journey or experience with the disease, a malady that affects nerve cells in the brain and spinal chord. The damaged nerve cells, in turn, cause problems with voluntary muscle movement, which causes atrophy.

The disease is progressive, but there have been cases in which it sort of arrests itself. There is no cure or even treatment, but there is one FDA-approved drug—Rilutek—that modestly slows the progression of ALS. And there are several other drugs that are still being tested and developed that hold promise.

Just as promising, for Duranko personally, has been the flood of support from his former Notre Dame teammates and former Irish coach Ara Parseghian.

"Ara helps me in ways he doesn't even know," Duranko said. "Everybody fails. Everybody, even Ara. But I saw Ara get back up every time in football and in life. And that's the biggest gift he gave me when I played for him and beyond."

Ironically, Duranko never envisioned himself at Notre Dame growing up in Johnstown—at least not without being coerced there. His father and mother never advanced beyond the sixth grade. The men who used to come cheer him at football games at Bishop McCort High School were often steel workers or coal miners. And those were the men he largely admired and pictured himself as one of.

But a priest at Duranko's grade school had a different vision. He kept pushing Duranko toward Notre Dame, even though Duranko had no idea where Notre Dame was or how he was going to lift his academic performance beyond a C-D level.

"It got to the point that every time I was supposed to get my grade card, the father would say, 'Where are you going to go to school?' And if I said, 'I don't know,' I wouldn't get the grade card," Duranko said. "He *made* me say Notre Dame, but after a while it worked. I started following their team and I started working harder on my grades. Still people told me I'd never make it there. I'd fail. I was very confused, but my high school coach—who was a big Penn State fan—told me I needed to shoot for the stars. He said, 'If you don't make it at Notre Dame, you can always transfer or go somewhere else. But if you don't go, you'll never be able to look yourself in the mirror, knowing you were afraid to try.'"

The Notre Dame football program that Duranko walked into wasn't anything like the one the priest had spoken about. It was the end of one of the darkest eras of Notre Dame football. Coach Joe Kuharich had come out of the pros with a closed mind and little idea how to relate to 19- and 20-year-old kids. Duranko's freshman season of 1962 represented the final season under Kuharich and the fourth non-winning season in a row for the Irish.

Notre Dame's fifth such season in succession, under interim coach Hugh Devore, unfolded in 1963 before Parseghian arrived and put Notre Dame back on college football's map in 1964. One of the reasons Parseghian was so successful was his ability to put players in the right spots. There were mass position changes, some of them rather stark.

Duranko was one of them—shifting from fullback to the defensive line. He had to wait until the 1965 season, though, to get on the field at his new position, because he suffered a broken wrist in preseason practice in 1964. That caused him to miss the magical turnaround season of 1964, but he was granted an extra year of eligibility, which allowed him to be a force in Notre Dame's 1966 title run.

He also became the first and only of the 10 Duranko children to earn a college degree. From there, it was on to the pros and seven seasons with the Denver Broncos (1967-70 and '72-74).

The desire to be with family, both Duranko's and his wife's, brought the couple and their two children back to Johnstown in the mid-'70s, but that made transitioning out of football much more difficult.

The local steel industry was in the throes of a collapse, and everyone in the southwestern Pennsylvania town felt it. Duranko tried to help his marketability by getting a master's degree in industrial relations and human resources at a nearby college. After graduating, he secured a job as a personnel manager at a small steel mill.

After two decades in that role, the plant shut down, and Duranko's life was adrift.

"I was 54, I had a master's degree, and nobody would hire me," he said. "They were always looking for somebody younger, but they'd never say that. I didn't want to leave Johnstown, but I couldn't find work for two years. Finally I decided to try to sell insurance. It was like a bad dream."

When Duranko awoke from his eight-hour heart operation on January 28, 2005, it no longer felt like a bad dream for some reason. Everything at least seemed to have its order and make some sense.

An aneurysm in his heart discovered fortuitously during a routine electrocardiogram had sent Duranko into the surgery, which was risky given the ALS, but there was no alternative.

As he lay in recovery, Duranko kind of reframed the events of the past few years. He got amusement from the fact that when he was finally diagnosed with ALS after two years of wondering and a year of tests and doctor visits, he was relieved. Relieved that he wasn't a hypochondriac.

He looked forward, too—forward to his 62nd birthday on December 15, 2005, forward to being a grandpa someday.

"I think my two sons are working on it," Duranko said. "They have cats."

This time Duranko welcomed the quiet. And in this quiet moment, there were no tough questions. Duranko was just happy to be alive and thinking of his next warped joke.

Where Have You Gone?

NICK EDDY

T he punches came at Nick Eddy in a flurry, but not once did the former Notre Dame All-America halfback think about swinging back or walking away.

That was five years ago during Eddy's second week on the job as a special education teacher in Modesto, California. The challenges have only grown more plentiful and extreme since for the 60-year-old, who, among other things, received death threats from one of his students last year.

"You come to realize that you have to pick your battles," said Eddy, a standout on Notre Dame's 1966 national championship team who currently teaches at Mark Twain Junior High School in Modesto. "And you also have to realize you're not going to save every kid. My goal is to help them learn some life skills that will help them better survive in society."

"Some of these kids have been dealt pretty tough hands—dads in prison, moms strung out on drugs, getting molested by mom's boyfriend, homelessness. You think, 'My God, life isn't supposed to be that difficult when you're 13, 14 years of age.' But then you break through with a kid. You give him confidence. You make him smile. You give him hope. That's why I'm here."

Colin Powell, according to Eddy, is also largely responsible for the Tracy, California, native's current vocation. The former Secretary of State and Chairman of the Joint Chiefs of Staff was on a book signing/speaking tour in the late 1990s when Eddy discovered Powell would be appearing a mere 15-minute drive away at a local college in Turlock, California.

Eddy and his wife were actually able to arrange a private meeting with Powell. They chatted with him, got their picture taken with him and then decided to stick around and hear him speak. And the message that resonated so pow-

#47

NICK EDDY

HALFBACK

PLAYING YEARS:
1964-1966

CLAIM TO FAME:
Unanimous All-American who was Notre Dame's leading rusher on its 1966 national championship team

HIGH SCHOOL:
Tracy High School

HOMETOWN:
Tracy, California

PROFESSION:
Special Education teacher at Mark Twain Junior High School in Modesto, California

CURRENTLY RESIDES IN:
Modesto, California

erfully with Eddy, a long-time insurance salesman at the time, was how kids need mentors.

"My wife and I talked about it," Eddy recalled. "We thought, 'Gosh, our kids are grown and well on their way into adulthood. At this point, maybe teaching is something I could do.' We started checking it out."

Eddy had no idea what subject he wanted to teach or what age group he wanted to work with, but special education never entered his mind. He spent a year as a substitute teacher trying to find those answers. And he attended classes at night, so he could start working toward certification.

"One day, a friend of mine, who is a junior high principal, needed some help with a class until he could get someone hired on a permanent basis," Eddy said. "It was a Special Ed class. That was my first exposure to it. They were kids who were behind two grade levels at the very minimum. Most of them were very emotionally immature. I had raised four kids of my own and know the trials and tribulations that kids go through. These trials were just more extreme. I came to realize this is where I could do the most good."

Since Eddy wasn't certified until the spring of 2005, job security was always an issue in those early years on the new job. If a certified teacher even applied for his job, he got bumped. So he bounced around until landing at Mark Twain Junior High in 2004.

"I still have another level of certification I'm just starting work on," Eddy said. "And that means more night school, but I'm fine with that. I'm not a youngster by any means, but I've got a little extra bounce in my step and have lots of energy. I'm just really enjoying it at a time when many of my colleagues are burnt out, tired, and very bitter."

Most of the students Eddy comes in contact with have no idea who he was before he came into their lives.

"I've never been one to wear my uniform around or my letterman's jacket or toot my horn that much," Eddy said. "That's just how I am."

The only clue to his past comes from the national championship ring he wears. That doesn't mean the memories aren't vivid and treasured.

"Timing is so much in life," said Eddy who was recruited by one of Notre Dame's least successful coaches, Joe Kuharich. After Kuharich abruptly resigned weeks after the signing period, Eddy ended up spending his freshman season (1963) under interim coach Hugh Devore, though freshmen were ineligible to play varsity ball during that era. He then spent three seasons under legendary coach Ara Parseghian, which included the 1966 title and a near miss in 1964.

"To be there when Ara Parseghian came in and kind of lit the fire and put the glare back on the Dome was probably the biggest thrill of all during my time at Notre Dame," Eddy said. "The fact that we did win the championship was probably icing on the cake."

Eddy was the leading rusher for the Irish in both 1965 (582 yards) and 1966 (553). He was a unanimous All-America selection in '66 and finished third in the Heisman Trophy voting behind Florida quarterback Steve Spurrier and Purdue signal-caller Bob Griese.

However, he didn't get a chance to play in the biggest game of the Irish 1966 national title run—No. 1 Notre Dame's 10-10 standoff with No. 2 Michigan State, perhaps the most famous tie in sports in the last 50 years.

Eddy had suffered a shoulder injury a couple of weeks earlier in a 38-0 rout of Pittsburgh, and reinjured it the next week against Duke.

"It felt like an electric shock going down my neck, shoulder and arm," Eddy recalled. "So they held me out of contact the next week in practice. Still somebody ran into me and aggravated it."

Eddy took a shot of cortisone the night before the team left for East Lansing, Michigan. His prospects for playing looked good until he went to get off the train. He slipped on a metal step, grabbed the rail and tore up the shoulder all over again.

"It was all muscular, so there was no danger of doing any permanent damage," Eddy said. "But the area of damage was so large and they had to shoot me up so much, my face went numb and I couldn't move my arms in warmups. So it was decided I couldn't play.

"That was one of the first games that was ever nationally televised. If I could have played in that game and had a decent game, I might have had a shot of winning the Heisman. Those are the type of things you look back on and ask, 'What if?' But it certainly didn't take away from the Notre Dame experience."

Nor did it dissuade the Detroit Lions of the NFL and the Denver Broncos of the AFL from making Eddy a second-round pick. He ended up playing five seasons for the Lions before moving into the business world in sales.

Eventually he and his wife got tired of shoveling snow and moved with their four children from Michigan to California. That was in 1979, and Eddy moved out of selling class rings, plaques and awards and into the insurance business.

"You know what's funny, I never go back to the Detroit Lions reunions," he said. "But I do go back to Notre Dame's. We seem to migrate together. We realize we had a unique experience that bonded us for life. As the years go by, you realize that bond—the fact that we care for each other, we're all good friends—was the secret ingredient of why we were successful."

Success requires a different formula for Eddy these days. Patience is the main ingredient.

Patience with the kids. Patience with himself. Patience with a system that has plenty of flaws.

"One of the most important things I've learned is that the system lets a lot of kids—I don't want to say fall through the cracks—but I think a lot of kids were not steered into programs that were best suited for their needs at the time, in the lower grades," Eddy said. "There are also a number of kids who you think, 'What is he doing in my class?' I don't want to use the term misdiagnose, because of the litigious society in which we live, but they have the abilities to move back into the conventional classrooms.

"But no matter why they're here, my job is to help. The young man who took the swings at me wasn't mad at me. He was mad at the world. And given his circumstances, how could he not be? But there's something special about each one of these kids. Every one has a chance. Every one has hope. Every one has worth. And it's my job to help them see that."

Where Have You Gone?

PAT EILERS

P at Eilers never questioned his father's advice that football wouldn't last forever. He just was hoping the end wouldn't occur so soon, during his sophomore year at Notre Dame.

Eilers had transferred in from Yale in the fall of 1986, had agreed to walk-on while trying to earn a scholarship and had spent his first fall in South Bend, Indiana, as practice fodder—playing scout team running back for Irish head football coach Lou Holtz's first Notre Dame squad.

Now here he was in the early days of spring practice in 1987 playing a new position (safety) and trying to get Holtz's attention. He did so, but not the type of attention he was hoping for.

During a drill Andy Heck, an eventual All-America offensive lineman, leveled Eilers. Holtz hardly helped him pick up the pieces, but he gave Eilers something much more valuable.

"He said to me, as only Lou Holtz can, 'You know Eilers, I'm trying to find a place where you can contribute,' " Eilers related. "And then he added, 'maybe you should have never transferred.'

"I think Lou's best attribute was maybe never allowing anyone to become complacent. So it didn't matter if you won the game. It didn't matter if you did it right yesterday. He always expected excellence, and there was a sense of urgency to always do your job. It's good enough, in a certain respect, to go out and do your best, but doing your best means you get it done. That's a pretty good lesson."

And one that the Chicago-area resident, husband and father of four carries with him to this day.

#13

PAT EILERS

WIDE RECEIVER/
STRONG SAFETY

PLAYING YEARS:
1987-1989

CLAIM TO FAME:
Transfer from Yale who
walked on to the team
and eventually became
a starting wide receiver

HIGH SCHOOL:
St. Thomas Academy
(Mendota Heights,
Minnesota)

HOMETOWN:
St. Paul, Minnesota

PROFESSION:
Financial partner for
Madison Dearborn
Partners in Chicago,
Illinois

**CURRENTLY RESIDES
IN:**
Chicago, Illinois

Eilers made the tackle the very next play, earned a scholarship by the end of spring and became a symbol of those players from early in the Holtz era that seemed to maximize every ounce of talent on the football field and every opportunity in life after football.

Today Eilers is a mover in the financial and investment world, working for Madison Dearborn Partners, a private equity firm in Chicago. Notre Dame is one of MDP's financial partners.

"I really love what I do, but this isn't what I originally thought I'd be doing after college," Eilers said. "I thought I was going to be a doctor."

Then again, the St. Paul, Minnesota, product was always pretty good about taking advantage of the Plan B's in his life.

Eilers was a running back for St. Thomas Academy in the mid-'80s, against the wishes of his father, Vincent—a Notre Dame grad and orthopedic surgeon in the Twin Cities—and drawing interest from a handful of Division I-A colleges. He was also a standout baseball player and a good enough skier to compete in the slalom at the Junior Olympics.

Midway through his senior football season at St. Thomas, though, Eilers suffered a broken collarbone. The big-time college football programs lost interest. Eilers was confused and crushed.

"I started giving the Ivy League more consideration," he said. "I thought, hmm, maybe that's the way Division I athletics worked. You get injured, they give up on you. I could have walked on somewhere, but I thought the Ivy League had a better perspective."

That notion didn't even stay with Eilers even for a full year. The doubts started chasing him at the end of his freshman football season, but he stuck it out for the rest of the school year. On the drive home from Yale's New Haven, Connecticut, campus to Minnesota, Eilers stopped at Notre Dame to attend his sister Anne's graduation ceremony.

He had also made an appointment to see Holtz.

"What had become evident to me about the Ivy League is that they sacrificed athletics for academics," Eilers said. "Usually you hear about it the other way around. I got to thinking that at a place like Notre Dame or Stanford, you could have the best of both worlds.

"People, at the time, tried to convince me that having a Yale degree would be good to have, but I thought I'd rather go to Notre Dame, give it a shot and never play than to stay at Yale, play a lot and graduate. I wanted to be able to look myself in the mirror and say I gave it a shot."

Eilers wasn't able to play in 1986 due to NCAA transfer rules. In 1987, after that pivotal first spring, he was a backup safety to George Streeter and a special teams stalwart. In 1988, Holtz moved Eilers to receiver, where he started seven games during Notre Dame's national title run. In 1989, he was a full-time starter at receiver. In Eilers's final two seasons, he played for the Irish baseball team as well.

His intangibles in football were more impressive than his stats. Eilers totaled 21 tackles, 11 receptions for 123 yards, 10 carries for 38 yards and four punt returns for 23 yards. His longest play in a Notre Dame uniform covered 20 yards. He scored one touchdown, a two-yard run in a 31-30 victory over Miami that knocked the Hurricanes from the No. 1 perch and pushed the Irish toward the top spot.

Yet Eilers was able to parlay his Notre Dame experience into a six-year NFL career (1990-95) as a defensive back. He was an undrafted free agent and had four offers. The Chicago Bears and New Orleans Saints wanted to bring him to camp as a wide receiver. Minnesota and the New York Giants liked him as a defensive back.

"I had good speed, but not NFL receiver speed," Eilers said. "Playing defensive back seemed like the smart way to go. Plus I had a girlfriend in the Twin Cities, who is now my wife."

Eilers spent his first two years with his hometown Minnesota Vikings. His third year, he spent training camp with the Arizona Cardinals. The Cardinals opted to keep another Notre Dame safety—Dave Duerson—and cut Eilers.

He was picked up later on in 1992 and played three seasons for the Redskins. He played his final pro season with Chicago. Every offseason, Eilers—who had two degrees from Notre Dame, in biology and mechanical engineering—worked in investing.

"My motivation to work outside of football was kind of twofold," he said. "Not being drafted, I didn't know how long football was going to last. The other thing was I wanted to set myself up for life after football. As my dad always said, it wasn't going to last forever."

That it lasted six years largely dissuaded Eilers from attending medical school. He had found a career he loved outside of football. He figured to specialize and become an orthopedic surgeon would be another eight to 10 years of training, and he somewhat had soured on the profession because of frustrations his father was having with the business.

"With all the HMOs that were cropping up, a lot of medical decisions were being made by the HMOs and business people as opposed to medical doctors," Eilers said. "It made it a much less attractive industry. So I walked away from that dream.

"But I walked away with no regrets. Life hasn't always turned out the way I thought it would. I've had to change directions, and fortunately I've had some options. All in all, though, I wouldn't change a thing."

JOEY GETHERALL

I t was during a punt return in the spring of 2003 that Joey Getherall's foot emphatically told him it was time to move on with life.

His heart was more than willing to go along for the ride.

For as much as the diminutive wide receiver had a passion for football, the first love for the 2001 Notre Dame graduate was always giving back to the community, to children, to people less fortunate than himself.

That is what eventually pushed the marketing major away from a possible career in college coaching, from lucrative business opportunities, from riding pro football's back roads for a few more years and coaxed him toward a career in law enforcement in the Los Angeles Police Department.

"Well it didn't hurt that my dad used to be in the LAPD," said Getherall, who completed his six-month training program in August of 2005. "And my sister [Tina] is in the LAPD as well as my godfather and two brothers-in-law. I guess it runs in the family.

"But more importantly, it's a chance to make a difference."

The pain in Getherall's foot turned out to be a torn ligament that eventually required two screws be inserted during surgery. Getherall, true to form, not only finished the game in which he was injured for the Amsterdam Admirals of NFL Europe, he finished out the season before having the injury checked once he got back to the U.S.

"It was a difficult injury to come back from," Getherall said. "I probably worked too hard in rehab. I tried to rush it and got tendinitis. I need my speed, and I just didn't have it."

Photo by Don Stacy

PLAYING YEARS:
1997-2000

CLAIM TO FAME:
Diminutive player
known for his big plays
and big heart

HIGH SCHOOL:
Bishop Amat High
(La Puente, California)

HOMETOWN:
Hacienda Heights,
California

PROFESSION:
Rookie cop in the Los
Angeles Police
Department

**CURRENTLY RESIDES
IN:**
Hacienda Heights,
California

Courtesy of Joe Getherall

Getherall limped through Indianapolis Colts camp in the fall of 2003, then sifted through some possibilities with the Canadian Football League before ending his brief run at pro football.

In the ensuing months, Getherall explored some business opportunities, got his real estate and real estate broker's licenses, and then got a taste of college football coaching.

Then-Utah head coach Urban Meyer, Getherall's position coach at Notre Dame, invited his former pupil to come stay at his house and soak up the atmosphere during the Utes' 2004 spring practice.

"Urban really tried to convince me to get into coaching," Getherall said. "I tried it for a week. I hung out with the coaches in their offices, went to the practices. And after a week, I knew it wasn't for me. I just couldn't deal with the coaching lifestyle.

"All the hours, all the stress, all the moving around, from job to job. I think it's tough on the family."

Ironically, it was Meyer who campaigned *against* Notre Dame recruiting Getherall out of Bishop Amat High School in La Puente, California, in the first place.

Getherall would lead Amat to CIF Division I state titles in both football and baseball. He would put up breathtaking numbers—his 24.2 yard-per-catch average as a senior led the state of California. He would garner the Olivers Award as the top Japanese-American athlete.

But he was five foot six, 145 pounds as a high school senior. And that scared more than just Meyer.

"I've had people hold that against me my whole life," Getherall said. "It doesn't bother me. My forte was speed. And when they looked at tape and saw me make play after play, that changed a lot of minds."

Wisconsin, Washington State, and Washington were Getherall's most likely college destinations until Notre Dame re-entered the picture. Jim Colletto, Notre Dame's offensive coordinator at the time, force-fed Meyer with game films of Getherall, and that finally opened Meyer's mind.

Once Getherall set foot on campus, Irish head coach Bob Davie became smitten with Getherall's combination of pluck and speed. But Meyer never passed along the message. In fact, he rode Getherall hard during those first fall drills.

"I thought he just hated my guts," Getherall said of Meyer. "He would say to me every day, 'You're never going to get on the field.' And I started thinking, 'Maybe I am never going to play here.' But later I found out he just was trying to get in my head to see if I'd crack. He was on me, because he wanted me to be ready to start my first game as a freshman, and I did end up starting that very first game."

Getherall had four catches for 57 yards in that debut against Georgia Tech in 1997. His impact off the field was even more impressive and almost as immediate. Soon Getherall was kick-starting reading programs at South Bend-area elementary schools by going to the schools and reading with and to the kids. He spoke to church youth groups. He spoke to high school sports teams. He took handicapped children bowling.

"I think when you're given a talent and you're in the spotlight, you have a responsibility to the people who look up to you," Getherall said. "When you first come to Notre Dame, you don't realize it. But when you see all the kids that wait for your autograph after the games and you see all the people who come just to watch you *practice*, you realize that you're a focal point of the community. Then I think it becomes your obligation to help that community. It helps them and it helps the Notre Dame name."

Getherall's name didn't become legendary during his four seasons at Notre Dame—all during the Davie era. But he did grow in stature (5-7, 175 when he graduated) and he did make a believer out of Meyer.

Injuries, including an abdominal problem that required surgery, limited his opportunities. Still, he did play in 41 games and start 13. His best season was his junior year, when he had 35 catches for 426 yards. As a senior, Getherall had a modest 17 catches, but he ranked ninth in the nation in punt returns (16.3 average). His 12.2 career punt return average ranks seventh in Irish history.

"I think the thing I remember most is running out the tunnel my first game and running out of it for my last game," Getherall said. "You think of all the great players who have done the same thing. The other thing I remember is all the smiling faces of the kids."

And that is what Getherall remembers about his father's days as an LA cop. The people who he helped stick out, not the perils.

"I know there are dangers with being in the LAPD—I'm not stupid," said Getherall, who plans to sell real estate on the side on his off-days. "But I don't think I ever worried one day about it when my dad was involved. I was just proud of who he was and what he stood for.

"Now it's my turn to stand for something. Now it's my turn to make a difference. Maybe that won't happen, but I refuse to believe that. So this is what I have chosen. This is what I want to do."

Where Have You Gone?

GARY GODSEY

T he phone message sounded more like a prank than a door opening. And given Gary Godsey's luck over the previous few months, it was a fair conclusion.

It was June of 2004, and the NCAA had not only rejected the Notre Dame tight end's petition for a sixth season of eligibility a month earlier, the collegiate sports governing body did it in such an untimely fashion that he missed an opportunity to be drafted in the NFL that April or even latch on as a rookie free agent in the days that followed the draft.

Godsey persisted for a while, hoping to slip in the NFL's back door somehow. He had tryouts with three NFL teams, but they each made it clear before the auditions that their rosters were already overflowing with players in whom they had invested weeks, even months of scouting. Still, Godsey monitored his voice mail religiously, just in case the most unlikely of scenarios led to a dream.

As he listened to the message over and over to gauge its authenticity that day, Godsey realized the NFL dream might never come back to life, but for the first time in a long time reality felt almost as good.

The articles generated from Godsey's plight with the NCAA caught the attention of a producer at Paramount Pictures. He saw the Tampa, Florida, product's picture on the Internet, reportedly embraced his story and called Godsey up to offer him a small part on the movie, *The Longest Yard.*

"I wasn't even sure I was going to call him back at first," said Godsey, who has a non-speaking role in the remake of the 1974 classic starring Adam Sandler and Chris Rock and released on May 27, 2005. "But I'm really glad I did. You could tell right away he was serious. Everything he promised, he delivered on. It

Courtesy of Joe Raymond

Courtesy of Gary Godsey

PLAYING YEARS:
2000-2002

CLAIM TO FAME:
Rose to become a start-
ing tight end after
being discarded from
the quarterback mix;
applied for a sixth year
of eligibility for the
2004 season, but was
rejected by the NCAA

HIGH SCHOOL:
Jesuit High

HOMETOWN:
Tampa, Florida

PROFESSION:
Recently completed his
master's degree in psy-
chology; also appeared
in the 2005 movie *The
Longest Yard*; examining
his options in acting,
football and business

**CURRENTLY RESIDES
IN:**
South Bend, Indiana

was a great deal. It was so good for me, because the NCAA thing really had my spirits down."

The six-foot-six Godsey is cast as a defensive end in the movie, wears No. 91 and plays a prison guard named "Malloy," an irony that was lost on everyone in the cast and crew but him. Notre Dame's president during Godsey's football career was the Rev. Edward A. Malloy. Godsey also performed as a double for some of the actors, and was even a stuntman on a play in which that particular character suffers a broken leg.

"It's kind of ironic, the guy I did the stunt for was playing tight end," Godsey said. "And I had to be careful, because the leg that got hit was the one with the bad knee."

The knee is healed now, but it was Godsey's left knee that started all the problems for him in the first place. He suffered a torn anterior cruciate ligament in Notre Dame's Gator Bowl loss to North Carolina State on January 1, 2003. After months of rehab, he was declared ready to resume his role as Notre Dame's starting tight end as a fifth-year senior, but during the August workouts he reinjured the knee and missed the entire 2003 season.

Maybe Godsey should have seen the injury coming—at least the first time. His father John's collegiate career at Alabama was cut short when he suffered a torn ACL in his left knee. Brother Greg, an offensive guard during his days at the Air Force Academy, also suffered a torn ACL in *his* left knee. And brother George, a former standout quarterback at Georgia Tech? Same injury, same ligament, same knee.

Only Godsey's mother, a former Junior Olympic swimmer, escaped the family curse.

"When I want to razz my dad, I tell him I got my athletic ability from her," Godsey said.

It's apparent he gets his perseverance from both of them. Godsey's parents encouraged him to apply for the sixth year, and he did so in December of 2003.

Sixth years are typically granted to players who have been sidelined two years or more due to injury. Godsey's original request was turned down in January of 2004 with the NCAA citing his redshirt year of 1999 being non-injury-related.

Godsey reapplied, citing extraordinary circumstances surrounding the injury, something that is covered in the NCAA's voluminous rulebook and a scenario that was not without precedent. Godsey's brother Greg, an Atlanta attorney, and father both jumped in to help. John Godsey cited statistics claiming that when an ACL is repaired, there is only a three percent chance of reinjuring it, and that in those rare instances the injury is typically the result of a football collision. Godsey's second knee injury came as a result of making a cut while running a pass route.

"I think I felt pretty good about my chances, because Notre Dame did," Godsey said. "And let me tell you, Notre Dame was so great about it. They hired a law firm in Indianapolis to handle it. They stood by me. But the process just kept dragging on and on. That was the hard part."

Notre Dame coach Tyrone Willingham opted to hold Godsey out of spring practices that year (2004), figuring that if the NCAA were to rule against him, it would be crueler to have let him go through spring practices. Then again, Willingham never dreamt the *entire* spring session would pass without a decision.

"It was horrible," Godsey said. "All I wanted to do was be out there."

Instead he was left with plenty of time to ponder his career at Notre Dame.

Godsey actually came to Notre Dame from Jesuit High School in Tampa hoping to be a college quarterback. Most of the schools that were recruiting Godsey preferred him at that position. Then-Notre Dame head coach Bob Davie preferred that Godsey play tight end, but he promised him Godsey could work with quarterbacks in the fall as a freshman.

Godsey was promptly moved to tight end in the spring of his freshman year, but was back at quarterback in the fall of 2000 as a sophomore. He actually opened the season as the No. 2 signal-caller behind option quarterback Arnaz Battle, then moved into the starting role in week No. 3 after Battle suffered a season-ending injury.

Godsey won his first start, a 23-21 triumph over Purdue—one of the schools that recruited him hard as a quarterback—then was displaced the following week by Matt LoVecchio, one of three true freshman backups on the roster. LoVecchio then started the balance of the season, while Battle eventually was moved to wide receiver and Godsey back to tight end.

Godsey's situation was typical of the quarterback chaos that characterized the Davie Era and spilled into Willingham's regime. Only one of the quarterbacks on the roster that season (2000) finished his career as a quarterback. That was LoVecchio, and he transferred to Indiana after his sophomore season following his displacement in the starting lineup by classmate Carlyle Holiday. In addition to Battle and Godsey switching positions, Jared Clark eventually became a tight end and Holiday a receiver.

"My dad and I talk almost every day about what kind of quarterback I could have been had I been given a real chance," Godsey said. "But it really was the wrong offensive system for me, and they didn't adapt their system to the style of quarterback I was. I mean, I was a pretty good quarterback in high school. I think I could have grown over my five years here, but I'm not going to complain. All I cared about was being a team player, and I think that's all I should have cared about at the time."

That's what made the NCAA decision hurt so much—not so much the possible NFL future it crimped, but the chance to be part of a team one more year, the chance to go out on his own terms.

"The NCAA is the biggest bureaucratic nightmare you could ever deal with," Godsey's father, John, said. "I've dealt with the IRS. I've dealt with a lot of different agencies. Nothing compares to this. There's no rhyme or reason. There's no due process. They wouldn't talk to us directly. They wouldn't take our phone calls. They say they stand for the student-athlete. Well, that's a bunch of bunk. Trying to figure out the NCAA is like trying to figure out a Rubik's Cube that's twice the size it's intended to be."

A year after the decision, John Godsey was still writing letters to the NCAA, said Gary, and still getting them back with vague, cryptic responses.

Gary himself pushed it aside months earlier and finished up his master's degree, fittingly in sports psychology, in May of 2005. He spent the previous semester working on the movie, which filmed in Santa Fe, New Mexico, and Los Angeles.

"I think when it is all said and done, I want to do something that puts together sports and business," said Godsey, whose undergraduate major was business. "I don't think I would want to be a clinical psychologist, but getting my master's in it sure helped me understand and process what happened to me."

A little less than a year after the movie producer called, a message on Godsey's voice mail again sounded more like a prank than it did a door reopening. This time, he didn't hesitate. The message was clear: there was a chance that the football dream was still alive. What's more, he received calls about two more film possibilities being in the works, though nothing was firm.

"I'm not sure what my future's going to look like, but I'm sure excited about it," Godsey said. "And in some ways, I'm very excited about my past. Even though things didn't finish the way I had hoped at Notre Dame, the important thing is the relationships that you build. I talk to Julius Jones, Glenn Earl, Jim Molinaro every day. I don't think it's that way at other schools. And when it comes right down to it, that's what I'm going to carry with me from Notre Dame for the rest of my life."

Where Have You Gone?

_____

MIKE GOLIC

M ike Golic still hasn't gotten used to the alarm going off at 4:30 a.m., even though it's been his morning ritual since 1998.

"I usually swear to myself before I get out of bed," the former Notre Dame outside linebacker from the Gerry Faust era said.

Shortly after five, he arrives at the ESPN studios in Bristol, Connecticut, for his national radio show, *Mike & Mike In The Morning*, that goes on the air at 6 a.m. EST. Almost like clockwork, broadcast partner Mike Greenberg is needling Golic about his waistline and his supposed love affair with Krispy Kreme doughnuts.

It's all in fun, and it's rather tame compared to some of the feedback Golic occasionally receives from listeners, including Notre Dame fans.

Especially Notre Dame fans.

"I love Notre Dame. I think it's the greatest school ever," Golic said. "But I also know my job, and my job says you can't be biased toward your school. You have to highlight the mistakes, just like you have to highlight the good things.

"I remember my dad told me way back when, he said, 'Always be yourself. If you put on an act for somebody, you're always going to have to do that. And people are never going to know if they're getting you or the act.' So I've always tried to be straightforward. You have to be able to call a spade a spade."

A more daunting challenge for Golic, both in his radio role and his TV appearances on ESPN's *NFL Live* show, was criticizing athletes.

"I've spent my whole life as an athlete and spent my life with athletes," said Golic, who went on to a nine-year NFL career after his playing days at Notre Dame ended. "When you walk out of that clubhouse and you start criticizing

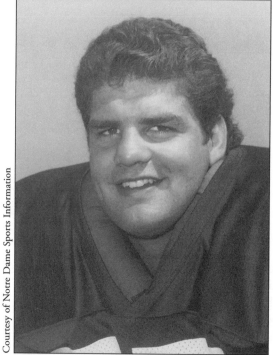

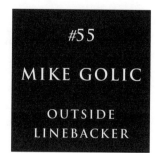

#55

MIKE GOLIC

OUTSIDE
LINEBACKER

PLAYING YEARS:
1981-1984

CLAIM TO FAME:
One of three Golic
brothers who played for
Notre Dame, Mike was
the first high school
senior to commit to the
Irish in the Gerry Faust
era

HIGH SCHOOL:
St. Joseph High
(Cleveland, Ohio)

HOMETOWN:
Willowick, Ohio

PROFESSION:
TV and radio personal-
ity for ESPN

**CURRENTLY RESIDES
IN:**
Avon, Connecticut

athletes, sometimes you are walking out of the fraternity of athletes. But sometimes you have to do it.

"That doesn't mean you have to be negative or get personal, but if somebody should have made a tackle or a block and they didn't, I have to point that out. I certainly have had players confront me, but if athletes want to get into this business, this is a hurdle you have to overcome—and probably the biggest one. If the time calls for it, you have to be able to be critical of athletes, and that includes people you played with and against."

Golic doesn't hesitate critiquing his own football career. In fact, the Willowick, Ohio, product is rather hard on himself—not for being the first player to commit to Faust. "Hey, I'm the answer to a trivia question," he said with a chuckle. Rather, he is critical of his decision to try to play through pain during his senior year (1984).

As a junior, Golic had risen to become Notre Dame's defensive MVP and an honorable-mention All-American. He was elected captain for the 1984 season, along with Larry Williams and Joe Johnson, and there was a buzz that the youngest of the three football-playing Golic brothers was playing himself into a first-round NFL draft choice, despite Notre Dame's chronic team mediocrity at the time.

But in the '84 season opener against Purdue, Golic went to take on a block from a pulling guard and got nailed underneath his shoulder pad.

"He absolutely smoked my shoulder," Golic said. "It was then that the upbringing from my dad kicked in: If you can walk, you can play. So I just kept playing."

At halftime, the team physician examined Golic, who tried to pretend he wasn't in pain. The doctor, sensing this, told Golic if he couldn't raise his arm above his head, he wouldn't be cleared to play in the second half. Golic tried unsuccessfully to make the required movement.

The doctor then turned to walk away. And when he did, Golic grabbed his wrist with his good hand and jerked his arm over his head. He called the doctor to turn around, and the ploy worked—for a while. Eventually, the officiating crew kicked Golic off the field when it was obvious he was essentially playing with one arm.

"Hindsight being 20-20, that's probably the biggest mistake of my football career," Golic said. "I continued to play in other games, too, the rest of the year, but I could barely play a half in any of them, because my shoulder hurt so much.

"I should have redshirted. I should have stopped playing, but I didn't want to. As a team, we hadn't been doing well my whole career, so coming back another year didn't sound too inviting. Plus, I think I had too high an opinion of myself. I thought I could go to the NFL combine and everybody would see how wonderful I was."

Golic never had a chance to shine at the NFL Scouting Combine. The shoulder injury required surgery, and he had not recovered sufficiently by the time the combine rolled around to either run or lift for the scouts.

He slipped all the way to the 10th round in the draft, three rounds beyond where today's draft concludes. Golic landed with the Houston Oilers, then broke an ankle and missed his entire rookie season.

"The tough thing wasn't making the team necessarily. It's that whenever you're a low-round draft pick, it's tough to lose that stigma," Golic said. "You're always kind of thought of that way, no matter what you accomplish on the field. And quite honestly, if you drop from the first round to the 10th round, it's going to cost you a few dimes."

It also made Golic have to work harder both as a pro football player and to get into the broadcast business.

"Steve Sabol, from NFL Films, always told me, 'Star players will always be given a job in the business,'" Golic said. "He said, 'A guy like you, people know you weren't a star, so you're going to have to keep working. And whenever you're asked to do something, you better be ready, because that's how you move up the ladder—hard work and preparation.'"

Fortunately for Golic, he grew up in the right house for that.

Golic's mother, Catherine, was a tireless worker in everything she did, including getting the boys involved in competitive swimming at a young age. Golic's father, Louis, was an ex-Marine and had played football at Indiana and in the Canadian Football League. By the time Mike was born, Louis had shunned offers to move into the NFL. Instead he became a bricklayer.

"He did it because he wanted to spend time with us," Golic said.

Although it wasn't always what outsiders might view as "quality time." As Mike and older brothers Bob and Greg were growing up, they would help their dad with side jobs on weekends.

"I was 12 years old, and I was swinging a sledgehammer—breaking steps or chimneys or driveways," Golic said. "And let me tell you, the first time you swing a sledge and break something, it's pretty cool. After about six hours of that, though, it starts to get old. But because of the way we were raised, we didn't view it like that. We didn't complain about it—at least not to his face. But that work ethic carried over to our sports. My dad passed it on to us, and I've passed it on to my kids. You're going to have to outwork your opponents. If you were going to do something, you understood what came along with it."

Bob was the first of the Golic brothers to attend Notre Dame (1975-78). He earned unanimous All-America honors as a senior linebacker in football and was a member of the 1977 national championship team. He was also one of the nation's top wrestlers while at Notre Dame.

His pro football career ran from 1979-92, after which he moved into television. Today he is a news talk radio host in Akron, Ohio.

"News and no sports? I don't know how he pulls that off," Mike Golic said, "but he loves it."

Greg arrived at Notre Dame at the end of the Dan Devine Era (1980), then played three years for Faust. The offensive lineman was a roommate of Mike's all three of those years. Today he is a computer designer and programmer.

"He's the smart one in the family," Mike said.

Mike arrived a year after Greg and met his future wife, Chris, on the first day of school while walking to a freshman orientation dance. Like Bob, he also wrestled, fashioning a 36-4-1 record in his sophomore and junior seasons in the heavyweight division.

"I think the official record says I lost six times, but I don't count the two losses in the NCAA Regional where my shoulder popped out," he said.

Mike Golic started easing into the broadcast business while he was still an active NFL player. He did a segment during Eagles quarterback Randall Cunningham's local TV show called *Golic's Got It*. The self-deprecating segment won an Emmy.

His first big break nationally came with ESPN when Golic had to interview a blind mountain climber as his first assignment. His career then began to pick up momentum and eventually he was asked to move from Scottsdale, Arizona, to Connecticut.

"That was a point of contention with my wife," he said. "I remember having to come to Bristol to do some stuff when I was playing, and I remember thinking, 'Oh my God, people live here?' But she forgives me now with each paycheck that comes."

And Golic's schedule leaves plenty of time to follow the athletic fortunes of his three kids—son Mike Jr. (a high school sophomore), son Jake (a freshman), and daughter Sydney (a sixth-grader).

"Other than that injury at Notre Dame and how I handled it, it's been a storybook deal that's been going on, and I'm really appreciative of," he said. "I've got a great wife, great kids, great career, and I wouldn't trade any of that or my time at Notre Dame.

"Honestly, when I signed with Gerry, I thought we were going to do well. And the second week of my freshman season we were Number 1 in the country. I thought 'Oh my God, this is how it's going to be.' And then the rug got pulled out, reality hit and we didn't fare that well. But that wouldn't have changed the fact I wanted to go there, because I loved the school then, and I love it every bit as much now."

Where Have You Gone?

SCOTT GROOMS

A modest 315 miles separate them now, though Art Schlichter is much further removed from Scott Grooms's mind.

The last time the two former quarterback prodigies spoke, Schlichter was briefly out of prison but still in a world of trouble. He wanted help from Grooms, financial help, to settle some gambling debts, though he certainly didn't frame it that way. Grooms knew better.

A former high school teammate of Grooms and a man who once followed a parallel dream had flushed a promising NFL career due to a gambling addiction. Schlichter filed bankruptcy in 1988, watched his marriage crumble six years later, but not before stealing and hocking his wife Mitzi's wedding ring.

In the decade that followed the breakup of his marriage, Schlichter spent time in 30 different prisons and jails. He was convicted of at least 10 charges related to fraud, forgery and theft. Weeks after contacting Grooms roughly five years ago, Schlichter became the target of an intense police manhunt. He eluded authorities for several days before being arrested at a diner in Ravenna, Ohio.

Schlichter's latest conviction was the upshot of a sports ticket scam in which he bilked 22 victims out of more than $500,000. He has been confined to a prison in Medaryville, Indiana, ever since, with a projected release date of May 28, 2008. He went 18 months between hugs from his two daughters. He missed the funeral of his father, Max, whose death in September of 2002 was ruled a suicide.

"Art and I were real close growing up, from the time we were in third or fourth grade," Grooms said. "It's a sad situation. Art was a great guy. I don't know what happened to him, but let's put it this way—Art is a sick, sick individual. I don't think he's ever intentionally hurt anyone, but he's damaged a lot of folks along the way. It's a sad, sad story, but unfortunately a true one."

Courtesy of Notre Dame Sports Information

PLAYING YEARS:
1980-1981,
1983-1984

CLAIM TO FAME:
Followed phenom Art
Schlichter as a starting
quarterback in high
school, then got lost in
a QB numbers game at
Notre Dame

HIGH SCHOOL:
Miami Trace High
(Washington Court
House, Ohio)

HOMETOWN:
Greenfield, Ohio

PROFESSION:
Insurance agent

**CURRENTLY RESIDES
IN:**
Granville, Ohio

Courtesy of Scott Grooms

Grooms's own story is not without potholes. His shoulder still aches—two decades after his playing career ended—despite five surgeries. His youngest daughter, now four, tests the lessons of patience Grooms learned as a quarterback at Notre Dame. And he still has trouble making sense of why his playing career never took off in South Bend.

But he has settled comfortably into life after football. Broken dreams still haunt him, but not to the point where he hasn't been able to embrace new ones. And never once since his college eligibility expired at the end of the 1983 season has Grooms regretted coming to Notre Dame in the first place.

"Do I think I could have played football after college if they had left me alone and let me play?" Grooms asked himself. "Absolutely. I'm not like some guys who didn't get the opportunity to play but know we were better than the guys in front of us. I wonder why, but I'm not bitter. I'm not one of those guys."

What Grooms is is a husband and father of two, living in Granville, Ohio—just beyond the urban sprawl of Columbus.

"I call it 'sophisticated country,'" he said. "We have a great school system and enough land to have horses, but we're close enough to Columbus to enjoy that life if we want to. It's the best of both worlds."

Within that world, Grooms has been in the insurance business for the past 18 years—the last five in rural Ohio.

Until the past couple of years, the bulk of Grooms's business had been insuring top college athletes around the country.

"I've done a lot of the high-risk Lloyd's of London-type stuff," Grooms said. "I still do a fair amount of it, but I've been transforming my business to work more with charities and universities.

"Quite honestly, I got tired of dealing with a lot of guys who are just a pampered bunch of idiots. Not the Notre Dame guys—they've always been a cut above, but there have been a lot fewer of them in recent years. But these other guys, you have to deal with them. And once they turn pro, you're dealing with their agents and their financial advisers. And they're bigger idiots than the athletes themselves. So it got to be a big pain in the butt.

"I still work with a few really good guys in the business, but I'm looking to build my business doing some other more mentally stimulating and more financially rewarding things when all is said and done."

Ironically, Grooms, the athlete, is just the type of client Grooms, the insurance agent, would likely have tried to cultivate as a client. Schlichter too.

"You don't necessarily insure first-round draft choices," Grooms said. "A guy like Justin Tuck at Notre Dame, who kind of came out of nowhere, for example, is not a guy we would have looked at. You have to be projected as a pro prospect early in your career. You have to see the potential very early."

In Grooms's case, then-Miami Trace High School coach Fred Zechman spotted the potential before Grooms had even learned his multiplication tables or cursive.

"I think I was in second grade and Art was in fourth when Coach Zechman handpicked us as the quarterbacks of the future," Grooms said. "He had Art and I work together all the time. By the time each of us were going into the seventh grade, we were going through two-a-days with the high school varsity. So I was kind of hardened, but at the same time very well-schooled."

Schlichter went from stardom in high school in Washington Court House, Ohio, to even bigger stardom up the road at Ohio State, usurping incumbent Rod Gerald at quarterback as a freshman under Woody Hayes and leading the Buckeyes to within an eyelash of the national championship in 1979 under first-year coach Earle Bruce.

Zechman followed Schlichter to OSU to join Bruce's staff in 1979 and he tried to recruit Grooms to go there.

"I wasn't a big fan of Earle Bruce," Grooms said. "Yet if Art had gone some-place else, I probably would have ended up there. I had sat behind Art before and kind of had been in his shadow. He was a good guy, a good friend and a hell of a teammate. But I wanted to make my own name somewhere."

UCLA, USC, Penn State, Michigan and Notre Dame got the strongest consideration. The atmosphere at a USC-ND game eventually sold Grooms on the Irish—as did a very real opportunity to play as a freshman.

As it turned out, a freshman quarterback did play extensively in the fall of 1980. But it turned out to be Blair Kiel, a highly decorated signal-caller in his own right from southern Indiana.

Grooms, however, said he was repeatedly told by Irish head coach Dan Devine and his staff that *he* was the team's No.1 quarterback, in name if not in playing time. In most weeks of the first half of that 1980 season, Grooms received the majority of the snaps in practice, only to end up a distant option in the games.

"Coach Devine kept telling me how much confidence he had in me, but that he couldn't throw me to the wolves right away," Grooms recalled.

Grooms's confidence soon began to wane. It only got worse when the Irish coaches tried to change his throwing motion. The good news, Grooms thought, was that Devine announced he would retire after the 1980 season. But the Gerry Faust regime brought only more heartache.

During Faust's first season (1981), he told Grooms that he wanted him to move to defensive back—a position at which Grooms at one time had earned all-state honors at Miami Trace.

"He didn't leave any choice," Grooms said. "He told me I was never going to play quarterback at Notre Dame. In retrospect, maybe moving to DB would have been the best thing for me, but I felt I never really got the chance at quarterback. I still felt I was the best one on the roster. I had been screwed with mentally and physically so much, I doubt I could have gone back to my high school and played."

Grooms went home to Greenfield, Ohio, and pondered his future. He ran into Schlichter, tossed the football around with him and even played some basketball, but he could tell they were living in different worlds. In the winter months of 1982, Schlichter was about to become a first-round draft choice—and fourth overall pick—of the Baltimore Colts. Grooms, meanwhile, was withdrawing from Notre Dame and looking to pick up the pieces at Miami of Ohio.

Grooms went through spring ball with his new team and performed well, but didn't hit it off very well with the coaching staff or his new teammates. He contemplated walking away from college for good—at least the football aspect of it.

In the summer of 1982, he was working at a mobile home plant for his uncle about a half hour drive from Notre Dame. He decided one day to stop over and work out with his old Irish teammates. And then he blurted out, loud enough for then-sports information director Roger Valdiserri to hear it, that he wished he could come back to Notre Dame.

Within moments Valdiserri produced Faust. And Grooms was back at Notre Dame in the fall.

He had the non-glamorous work of running the scout team offense in the fall of 1982 and he had to pay his own way that semester because Miami would not give him his release to transfer initially. By the time Grooms returned for his final season in 1984, he had logged just 17 minutes and 43 seconds of playing time and had thrown five passes—all incomplete.

His final year, though, he did get into three games, completing 14 passes in 39 attempts for 134 yards, one interception and his only collegiate touchdown.

When Grooms returned to southwestern Ohio after graduation, Schlichter has already begun the downward slide. The NFL had taken football away from him, suspending him for gambling. Grooms, meanwhile, pushed football away and looked for a job in the business world.

"Art and I were growing apart each year," Grooms said. "In fact, I really lost touch with most of my friends from high school. The lasting friendships I have now are those I made at Notre Dame. And that's one of the reasons I am so glad I came back.

"What happened to me from a football standpoint at Notre Dame could have happened anywhere. Sometimes getting to the top of the depth chart has mostly to do with politics. Sometimes it's being in the right place at the right time. I'm not sure both of those weren't working against me. And there's still no doubt in my mind I was the best quarterback there when I was at ND.

"But that's not what I hold onto. I hold onto the fact that a poor farm boy from Ohio got to go to New York City, California, Hawaii, Miami. I got to travel and do things most kids don't have the opportunity to do. I got my education paid for. I got a chance to make the kind of life I dreamed about. Who could look back and be bitter about that?"

Where Have You Gone?

JEROME
HEAVENS

T he tears rolled down Jerome Heavens's cheeks for hours, from the time he shifted the car out of park in the Chicago Bears' training camp parking lot in Lake Forest, Illinois, until he crossed the Mississippi River into St. Louis's city limits 315 miles later.

No one ever told the man who had broken the legendary George Gipp's 58-year-old career rushing record at Notre Dame in the fall of 1978 just why his pro football career had been reduced to little more than an audition and a shove out the door less than a year later.

"Maybe I was a 'tweener," Heavens reflected on the end of his playing days. "Maybe I wasn't big enough to be a fullback. Maybe I wasn't blazing fast enough to be a halfback. Maybe I was before my time."

Whatever the reason, the end hurt. Not because Heavens didn't have a Plan B. Not because this represented the shattering of his own dreams. It was the dreams he carried for other people that concerned Heavens, that reduced him to sobbing for hours that late summer day in 1979.

There was Sister Angela Eichensehr, the nun who had such a profound impact on Heavens as a seventh- and eighth-grader and who taught Heavens as much about confidence as humility. There were the kids whose lives he touched as a substitute teacher in St. Louis and across the river in his hometown of East St. Louis, Illinois, in between graduation day in December and draft day in the spring.

There were all the people at Notre Dame who were pulling for him—everyone from university president the Rev. Theodore M. Hesburgh to head coach Dan Devine to Heavens's freshman guidance counselor, Emil T. Hoffman.

#30

JEROME HEAVENS

FULLBACK

PLAYING YEARS:
1975-1978

CLAIM TO FAME:
Broke George Gipp's
career rushing mark at
Notre Dame in 1978

HIGH SCHOOL:
Assumption High

HOMETOWN:
East St. Louis, Illinois

PROFESSION:
Sells beer for an inde-
pendent distributor in
Chicago

**CURRENTLY RESIDES
IN:**
Lansing, Illinois

Most of all there were his parents—mom a cashier, dad a fireman—who sacrificed everything for their children to escape a public school system ravaged by seemingly annual teacher strikes and the largely abject poverty of the city itself.

"I felt like I not only let the people from Notre Dame down, but everyone who had ever believed in me, taken a chance on me—and that's why it hurt so much," Heavens said of his abbreviated affair with pro football. "I had prepared myself to go into the business world and I knew that things don't always go your way.

"But you're driving in the car and you can't stop crying, because you wonder what those people think about you. I guess as you grow and get older, part of maturing is that you don't worry about what other people think of you. The bottom line is what you think of yourself. You pick up the pieces and move on."

Heavens is so far removed from the spotlight that once was so kind to him, most people he encounters don't even believe he played football at Notre Dame, much less etched his name all over the Irish record book.

"They try to test you," Heavens says with a laugh. "They say, 'Well, do you know Rudy?' Well, of course I do. One-play Rudy was a teammate of mine, and God bless him for who he is and the message he delivers about getting up when you're knocked down. But they're more impressed that I know Rudy than the fact I once held some records there. So I don't bring it up unless it's a real deep conversation."

Mostly Heavens talks about beer. Budweiser Beer, to be precise.

He sells Budweiser in the Chicago area for an independent distributor called City Beverages. That's akin to trying to sell Notre Dame merchandise outside LA Memorial Coliseum during a USC game.

"Old Style is the No. 1 brand in Chicago, and Chicago people are very loyal," Heavens said. "That's what makes this particular job challenging. I could have stayed in St. Louis, where Anheuser-Busch had like a 60 to 70 percent share. I guess I just have a competitive edge from my days at Notre Dame. When I first got here 25-26 years ago, I think we had a five or six percent share. Now I think it's up to around 30. That gives me a lot of pride, but I took a lot of bumps and bruises along the way."

But if Sister Angela Eichensehr could see Jerome Heavens today, she would see that her hopes and dreams for one of her most prized pupils came true anyway—bruises and all.

Heavens does not live a glamorous life or an especially financially lucrative one in Lansing, Illinois. But he has become the father, husband, and son all those people who emotionally invested in him could be proud of. And he has never forgotten the people who helped give him his happily-ever-after, even if it didn't include pro football.

"It didn't take me years to realize how much my parents did for me," Heavens said. "I saw how far the students fell back every time there was a strike in the public schools. My parents sent me to a place where family doesn't mean just people who you're related to, but to a place where strangers learn to love you.

"For all the other people, I thank them in my own way, and my way is to say prayers for them and just keep a positive outlook on things. Part of that outlook, a large part, comes from being at Notre Dame. That Notre Dame experience was one of the greatest things that could have happened to me, even if people don't remember me anymore."

Heavens's career rushing mark didn't even last a year. Teammate Vagas Ferguson broke it during the very next season, and Heavens now stands fifth on the all-time rushing list. Another mark, the Notre Dame freshman rushing record, did stand for 29 years—until Darius Walker erased it at the tail end of 2004 season.

"He's a different style of runner," Heavens said of Walker. "And he got an extra game, the bowl game, to break it, but I have to say I was pulling for him. I'm Notre Dame's biggest fan, I really am."

So much so that on Thursday nights, Heavens puts a blank piece of paper on the refrigerator for his wife to list his honey-do projects to perform on Friday.

"I'll do anything and everything on Friday," he said. "But come Saturday, I say, 'Don't bother me.' It's all Notre Dame football. I'm here for them.

"Even when I played, it was all about team. I did tell my dad I was going to break the record someday when I was still at Assumption High, but I really didn't care about the records. Records are made to be broken. Teams are forever. All I ever wanted to do was blend in.

"My first carry at Notre Dame was a fumble—then I *really* wanted to blend in," Heavens said with a laugh. "But you pick yourself up and keep going. People are there to love and support you. You just make sure you do the same."

Where Have You Gone?

SKIP HOLTZ

E very time Skip Holtz sees his mother's smile, every time one his children shows some perseverance they must have learned from "Nanny," he relishes all over again the professional detour he took for six years.

"If you looked at it from a professional growth standpoint, I don't think you could look at it as a very smart move," said Holtz, who left as the head coach of a burgeoning Connecticut football program after a 10-win season in 1998 to become offensive coordinator under his father at a dilapidated South Carolina program.

"Financially, it wasn't a very intelligent move, either. And initially I wasn't going to go. But my wife said, 'Twenty years from now, when your parents are gone, are you going to regret not going?' And I said that I would. And she said, 'Well, then we need to go.' Six years later, was I glad I went? My kids got to grow up in the same neighborhood as Nanny and Papa. So, yes, because for all the reasons I went, those are still there."

Even though he took a pay cut. Even though South Carolina reneged on its promise to promote Skip to head coach when Skip's father, Lou Holtz, retired as the Gamecocks' head coach. Even when Lou diluted Skip's offensive coordinator duties in a massive staff makeover heading into the 2004 season.

To this day, Lou Holtz wonders aloud if the presence of Skip, wife Jennifer and their three children (Louis III "Trey", Chad and Hailey) didn't have as much to do with Beth Holtz being cancer-free in 2005 as anything else.

Beth, Lou's wife, was battling throat cancer when the elder Holtz bitterly parted ways with Notre Dame after the 1996 season—his 11th as the Irish head football coach. After the families moved to Columbia, S.C., the cancer spread to Beth's liver, lung, adrenal gland and ovary.

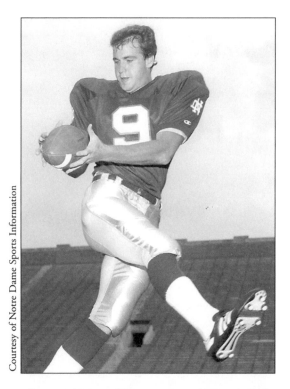

Courtesy of Notre Dame Sports Information

#9

SKIP HOLTZ

WIDE RECEIVER/
SPECIAL TEAMS

ECU Athletic Media Relations

PLAYING YEARS:
1986

CLAIM TO FAME:
The son of legendary
coach Lou Holtz who
has made a name for
himself in the college
coaching profession

HIGH SCHOOL:
Fayetteville High

HOMETOWN:
Fayetteville, Arkansas

PROFESSION:
Head football coach at
East Carolina
University

**CURRENTLY RESIDES
IN:**
Greenville,
North Carolina

"She went through a very aggressive treatment program for two years," Skip said. "That really kind of physically wiped her out. She spent a lot of time in bed, very little time awake. It did a lot of damage to her throat, a lot of scar tissue. She lost her saliva glands, taste buds, things like that. But she's doing very well these days, considering. She's a very strong woman."

And every bit the influence in Skip's life that his famous father has been.

"She's a very quiet woman," Skip said. "She's not an attention person. She doesn't want to be the center of attention or in the media or in the limelight or on TV. That's not her. She's a behind-the-scenes woman. She's an incredibly religious woman. I think she is the glue to this family."

Beth Holtz has certainly helped hold together Skip's dreams.

Where those dreams have taken him after Lou's retirement is to Greenville, North Carolina, where he is the head coach of East Carolina University. The once-pesky mid-major under Bill Lewis and Steve Logan lost 23 of 26 games before Skip took over following the 2004 season.

"I think everybody in the back of their minds thinks about where they hope to end up," said Skip, who counts fellow Notre Dame grads Greg Hudson and Thomas "Rock" Roggeman among his assistant coaches. "And like a lot of people, I would love someday to have the opportunity to coach my alma mater. The difference is, a lot of other people have a dream to coach at my alma mater.

"But I don't say that in a negative light about East Carolina. I'm not looking to jump on the first train out. I always felt the best way to further yourself is to take care of the job you have. I think people who are always trying to get another job normally aren't the ones who are very successful. Another thing I've learned is who you're working with is 10 times as important as where you are. And the leadership of Chancellor [Steve] Ballard and athletic director Terry Holland really jumped out at me."

Skip, born Louis Leo Holtz Jr., knew he wanted to be a leader himself from a very early age. The second oldest of the four Holtz children and the only one who migrated to college athletics also knew he wanted to attend Notre Dame as a student someday, just as his father had wanted to.

But just as his father was, Skip was denied admission. Lou ended up at Kent State, but Skip wasn't about to give up. Average grades and the lack of foreign language requirement were what was holding up the younger Holtz.

He decided to visit Notre Dame anyway while a junior at Fayetteville (Arkansas) High School. He met with Gerry Faust, the Irish head coach at the time, and men's basketball coach Digger Phelps.

"What they told me was Holy Cross Community College in South Bend was a great channel for me to transfer into Notre Dame," Skip said. "So many times when you go to another school with the intent of transferring, you lose your focus of what you're trying to get done, and you don't make the grades. At Holy

Cross, every day when you pull out from class, you're looking at the Golden Dome. You see your goal very day."

Skip transferred to Notre Dame after two years. Meanwhile, his father had moved on from Arkansas and was reviving a moribund Minnesota program when the idea of coaching converted from an option to a dream for Skip. During the 1985 season, in fact, Skip made up his mind that he would approach Faust about walking on in the spring. Skip figured playing at the college level, no matter how modest the role, would accelerate his coaching aspirations.

However, Faust was struggling, and at the end of the '85 season, he resigned. The new coach was Lou Holtz.

Skip had been a quarterback at Fayetteville High, but only had walk-on offers from a handful of colleges and knew his limits. He began spring practice as a quarterback, but quickly converted to flanker.

His best collegiate game turned out to be the Blue-Gold intrasquad game in the spring, in which Skip had three receptions for 54 yards. Once fall came around, Skip did not catch a pass in a game and had only one carry for one yard. But he did play in all 11 games on special teams and gained some valuable insight that would help him later in coaching.

He also got a taste of what it would be like to work for his father by playing for him.

"I kind of knew what I was getting into, because I knew how driven Coach Holtz was," Skip said. "When he got upset with me, I didn't go, 'Wow, that's a side of him I never saw.' He did that when I was 16, too. I think the part that was an adjustment for me and the part that was hard for me to understand is that he was a lot harder on me than he was everybody else.

"I understand it now—just from an acceptance type of thing, he had to be hard on me. I remember missing a meeting, and my punishment was harder than anyone else's. He told me, 'You know, there were eight of you who missed that meeting, but you're my son. You know better.'"

Skip found himself back at Notre Dame in the fall of 1990 after spending two seasons as a graduate assistant coach at Florida State under Bobby Bowden and one as an assistant coach under Earle Bruce at Colorado State.

He coached receivers for two years (1990-91) at Notre Dame before Lou went shopping for an offensive coordinator.

"He offered it to Joe Moore first, but Joe turned him down, because he saw himself as an old line coach, not a coordinator," Skip said. "He then asked me if I knew who'd make a great coordinator. I told him that I'd really like to have the opportunity, but he said he couldn't do it at that time with me being his son.

"Then I told him Mark Richt at Florida State. When Coach Holtz called Coach Bowden to ask permission to speak with Mark, Coach Bowden told him only if he could hire me if Coach Holtz hired Mark. So Coach Holtz said, 'Well if I'm just going to switch coaches, I might as well hire Skip.'"

The Irish went 21-2-1 in Skip's two seasons as coordinator, and their No. 3 national ranking in total offense in 1991 represents the best Irish standing in that category in the past 35 years.

From Notre Dame, Skip went to Connecticut—the school Lou Holtz was coaching at as an assistant when Skip was born. Skip went 34-23 in five seasons with the Huskies, who continued their ascent even after Skip left.

"The experience of being a head coach before at Connecticut has been invaluable here at East Carolina," Skip said. "I made an awful lot of mistakes in my first year at Connecticut. I think you can be an assistant for 20 years, and it doesn't prepare you for what you're going to have to do as a head coach.

"Going back to being an assistant, at South Carolina, was tough, especially for as long as it lasted. You have that professional itch inside you, and you can't scratch it. But my mom taught me so many lessons about the power of family. It's a tremendous gift. I know what's important in life. And that never changes."

Where Have You Gone?

JOE HOWARD (JOHNSON)

J oe Johnson walked out onto the practice field on August 8, 2003, hoping to
see an answered prayer.

Sixteen varsity football players greeted the new head coach at Archbishop
Carroll High School in Washington, D.C., that afternoon. *Sixteen*, in varying
stages of football shape and legitimate interest.

Suddenly Johnson's heart stopped racing and fell into his stomach. His mind
started running through the scenarios of innocent mistakes that could have
accounted for the low turnout.

This, after all, was Johnson's alma mater, a school that launched promising
careers for him in two sports—football and basketball—at Notre Dame two
decades earlier when he was known as Joe Howard. This was the school Joe's
father, Joseph Johnson Sr., had sacrificed his family life for so that young Joe
could have a better life. This was a school that could win games on its reputation back in the late 1970s.

Now, not only were the wins gone, so were the alumni contributions. The
pool of potential students whose families who could metabolize the $7,100-a-
year tuition without tremendous hardship had become a puddle. And why
would they want to try?

Facilities at Carroll had become outdated. The athletic program was in deep
rot. The school's tradition had grown weeds.

Johnson himself had given up a comfortable job with the CIA to chase this
coaching dream of sorts.

"It wasn't anything exciting or sneaky," the former wide receiver/point guard
said of his years with the CIA that overlapped his on-again, off-again pro foot-

#24

JOE HOWARD (JOHNSON)

WIDE RECEIVER

PLAYING YEARS:
1981-1984

CLAIM TO FAME:
Not only did he finish his career as Notre Dame's fifth all-time leading receiver, he filled in at point guard on a depleted 1983-84 Irish hoops squad and became one of the most storied walk-ons and beloved figures in ND basketball history

HIGH SCHOOL:
Archbishop Carroll High
(Washington, D.C.)

HOMETOWN:
Clinton, Maryland

PROFESSION:
Head football coach at Archbishop Carroll High School; also works in the attendance office at the school

CURRENTLY RESIDES IN:
Dumfries, Virginia

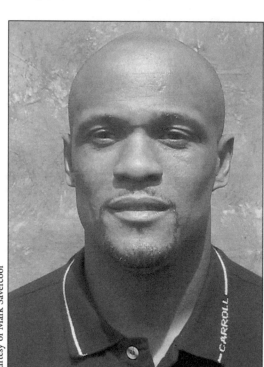

ball career. "I was in personnel with the Agency. It was a way to pay the bills and nothing more."

Coaching, though, was a passion.

"Actually, I wanted to coach basketball initially," said the husband and father of four. "But I thought my opportunities would be better in football, because I had played in the NFL. But even those were hard to come by. Every one I applied for, I got turned down.

"I don't want to say I was full of myself, but with the credentials I had, it didn't make sense. But I'm a Christian, and I really believe it wasn't God's plan for me to have those jobs. I said, 'God, you put me where you want me to be.' The next day Carroll called."

Johnson knew Carroll had an opening, but it was the *one* place he didn't apply. He, in fact, didn't even send his own children to school there.

"I knew the program had slipped," Johnson said. "I just didn't realize how far. I didn't know if I could work that hard. I didn't know if it could be saved. I didn't think it was my plan, but God sometimes has different ideas."

Carroll won one game that first year under Johnson, but by the end of the season, the roster had swelled to 39 kids. In year two, the roster numbers and the victories increased impressively. The varsity went 4-6. Johnson started a JV program, and it went 2-3. Most impressive was the freshman team that fashioned a 5-2 record.

The triumphs off the field were the biggest, though.

"I'm trying to instill a sense of pride in the school and in the players themselves," Johnson said. "I'm trying to teach them to believe in themselves, believe that they can go to college, believe they can go out and change the world. They need to know their lives aren't headed for a dead end."

Johnson could have had the same misconception about life, but his grandfather, McClellan Johnson, and uncle David Johnson made sure that didn't happen.

In his early years, Joe lived in the same house with those two along with 12 aunts. He had enough logistical challenges trying to figure out how to survive at the dinner table and occasionally worm his way into the bathroom amidst the jungle of curlers and lipstick without having to come to terms with what Vietnam was and why he could never see his daddy.

It was Uncle David who first showed Joe how to juke a defensive back on the football field and how to double-pump in traffic amidst the tall timber on the basketball court. It was McClellan who came to every game in every sport, even when Joe Johnson Sr., returned from the war in Vietnam.

Young Joe, who had taken on his mother's maiden name (Howard), moved in with his unmarried parents when his father finally came home.

"I still didn't see my dad much, though, because he was a workaholic, and I mean that in a respectful way," Joe said. "He was a provider. He showed me what work ethic was, and he made a lot of sacrifices for me. I knew he loved me."

Joe's mom, Barbara, practiced tough love. After Joe's sophomore year in high school, she would not allow Joe to play sports if his report card wasn't filled exclusively with As and Bs. He got his only C during the third quarter of his senior year, and true to her word, Barbara pulled Joe off the track team.

She also was the person who directed him to Notre Dame.

Joe actually had far more scholarship offers for basketball than he did for football, and basketball was his first love, but he chose football, because he figured there were far more five-foot-nine players in the NFL than there were in the NBA.

Coach Gerry Faust's staff at Notre Dame was among the football suitors. And Joe was open-minded to that possibility until he took his recruiting visit to South Bend, Indiana.

"If I was 150 pounds soaking wet at the time, that would have been generous," Joe recalled. "When I got to Notre Dame, all the other guys who were visiting were big. And the Notre Dame coaches offered every one of them a scholarship except for me. So of course, when I got home, I said, 'Well, I'm sure not going there.'"

He committed to North Carolina shortly thereafter, but Notre Dame assistant Greg Blache showed up on signing day hoping to change Joe's mind.

"I was prideful and told him I wasn't interested," Joe said. "That's when my mother stepped in and said, 'Excuse me' and took me upstairs. She told me she didn't care what happened on my recruiting trip, I was going to go to Notre Dame. I tried to protest, and she wouldn't hear it. The only thing she promised me was that if I didn't like the school, I could transfer to North Carolina."

It took all of a couple of weeks for the transfer pangs to surface. Joe began practicing with the tailbacks initially and soon found himself as the ninth option at that position.

"I was calling home every day," he said. "I told my mom, 'I ain't never heard of a place where you've got eight people in front of you.' She told me I better not come home. I reminded her of our deal, though. And then she asked me how I liked the school. I told her that I loved the school. The school wasn't the problem. The problem was football.

"She said, 'Well, I didn't send you there to play football. I sent you there to get an education and a degree.'"

Joe did those things as well as leaving school as Notre Dame's fifth all-time leading receiver after changing positions and shooting up the depth chart. He also became one of the more beloved figures in Irish *basketball* lore.

During Joe's junior year, Notre Dame men's basketball coach Digger Phelps approached Howard about walking on to the team. Nicknamed "Small

Wonder," Joe joined the hoops squad in early January, a week after the Irish football team concluded its season in the Liberty Bowl.

Howard, one of only four Division I players who pulled the football-basketball double duty in 1983-84, saw action in all 23 games from that point forward and started 11 times. He scored 14 points in his collegiate debut against Holy Cross and a career-high 15 against Pitt in the NIT with 12 assists. He stands second only to Willie Townsend in single-season scoring among Notre Dame walkons.

"I thought I knew it all about basketball when I got to Notre Dame," Joe said, "but I learned so much from Digger. And I played some of the best basketball of my life. I had such a good time—not many people know this—but I almost quit football. It got to the point me and Coach Faust didn't see eye to eye on anything. He didn't like me playing basketball. We had a meeting, and there were things that were said that stuck with me so long.

"The next year I had a reduced role in football. I think that's a big reason I didn't get drafted."

Joe didn't play basketball his senior year in part to get ready for the draft and in part because Phelps had recruited a point guard prodigy named David Rivers.

The first pro camp Joe attended was Tampa Bay's, and he got cut, so it was then he started working for the CIA. He worked there every offseason, even though he stuck with football until the mid 1990s. His most productive years were as Joe Howard with Buffalo and Joe Johnson with Washington.

"My parents got legally married when I was a sophomore in college," Joe said. "At that time, I changed my named to Joe Howard-Johnson legally, which was kind of confusing because my roommate was a defensive back named Joe Johnson. We just answered the phone 'Howard Johnson's.' I kept wearing Howard on the back of my jersey, but when I came back home to Washington, it was time to honor the family name."

Joe carries the name and the lessons of his childhood proudly.

Those lessons come in handy when he's filling out paperwork in his free time, trying to get an underprivileged student-athlete financial aid or when he has to work 'til two or three in the morning on a fund-raiser for Archbishop Carroll.

"I pray a lot in those moments," he said. "My grandpa taught me that. He made me go to church, and I didn't understand that as a kid. But I do now. I also know what it's like to see a prayer answered. I know what it's like to be blessed."

Where Have You Gone?

ANTHONY JOHNSON

E very once in a while, Anthony Johnson thinks about Fred Lane. He remembers what a tortured soul Lane was when the two of them first became friends while teammates in the late 1990s with the NFL's Carolina Panthers, how Lane's off-the-field turmoil threatened to consume his on-the-field brilliance.

Johnson just as vividly remembers the spring day in 2000 when Johnson's child and Lane's child were playing soccer together at a local church in the Charlotte area, and Lane came running up to Johnson to tell him he had bought a Bible and joined a church and that he was committed to stop inflicting scars on his own soul.

"I've never seen a smile like that in all my life," said Johnson, a former Notre Dame running back in the late 1980s. "When he told me how committed he was, and you could see he was sincere about it, I teared up a little bit. I knew at that point I wanted to have that kind of effect on other people's lives. That's a big part of what drove me then and still drives me today."

Today Johnson is the team chaplain for the NFL's Jacksonville Jaguars, the same team with which the South Bend, Indiana, product finished his 11-year NFL career. He executes chapel services, runs a weekly Bible study and meets one on one with players anytime they have an issue—spiritual or otherwise—that they would like help with.

"The whole NFL has chaplains now, all 32 teams," said Johnson, who took the position with Jacksonville in 2003. "Personally the most rewarding thing is to know all my energies and efforts occupationally are tied to the call that God has placed in my life. And to see the guys' eyes open to the Word and see their faces when it clicks. However small that is, that's the part of the process I enjoy."

Michael and Susan Bennett/Lighthouse Imaging

Courtesy of Rick Wilson

ANTHONY JOHNSON

FULLBACK

PLAYING YEARS:
1986-1989

CLAIM TO FAME:
One of the more versatile and underrated players in the Lou Holtz era; started six games and got married during Notre Dame's 1988 national title run

HIGH SCHOOL:
John Adams High School

HOMETOWN:
South Bend, Indiana

PROFESSION:
Chaplain for the NFL's Jacksonville Jaguars

CURRENTLY RESIDES IN:
Jacksonville, Florida

Johnson wonders now where the process would have taken Fred Lane. How many lives could he have changed? How many hearts could he have soothed?

Lane was shot to death on July 6, 2000, three months after running into Johnson at the soccer field. He was 24 years old. Lane's wife, Deidra, is serving seven years, 11 months in prison after pleading guilty to voluntary manslaughter.

Deidra, whose own troubled past included previous jail time, alleged that physical abuse by Lane led her to that point. The prosecution called that fiction and alleged the killing was motivated by a $5 million insurance policy on Fred Lane. The judge, who imposed the maximum sentence, couldn't get past the fact Deidra walked through Fred's blood to shoot him in the head after she had already mortally wounded him with a gunshot to the chest from five feet away. He had just walked in the door from an out-of-town trip.

"The only sense you can make of it from a spiritual standpoint," Johnson said, "is that it was time for God to bring His child with Him, which is good. It was also good that Fred had taken this step as His child to really start to walk with Him. But from a human or earthly standpoint, the ridiculousness of what his wife did, I'll never understand.

"It's also something I'll never forget. Sometimes I see him in the faces of some of the guys I counsel."

Johnson's own faith journey started at a young age. His dad died when he Johnson was six years old. The family had just started attending church shortly before his passing.

"By the time I was eight, I had come to an understanding of who Christ was and what He had done," Johnson said. "Ever since then, I have been drawn to God and His Word and the understanding of Him."

But that didn't keep Johnson from straying. From the time Johnson was a junior at Adams High School in South Bend until the middle of his sophomore year at Notre Dame, Johnson talked the talk, but he didn't live it.

"I was partying, running around chasing girls, the whole deal," Johnson said.

In the interim he ended up at Notre Dame almost as a fluke. Gerry Faust was the Irish head coach when Johnson was a high school senior. He offered Johnson the opportunity to walk on, as Johnson's older brother Mike had done, but no scholarship would be extended.

"It really then came down to Stanford and Michigan, which had both offered me scholarships," Johnson said. "I had finally decided on Michigan and was all set to go there, when there was a coaching change at Notre Dame.

"It's my understanding the new coach, who was Lou Holtz, mistakenly thought Gerry had offered me a scholarship. So he asked me to come visit, and then he offered me a scholarship. I was surprised. I was thrilled. And I stayed home and went to Notre Dame."

Johnson was never brave enough to ask Holtz if his portal to Notre Dame really was the result of a misunderstanding, but it sure turned out to look purposeful. Johnson went on to become a versatile threat, who could block, run between the tackles, turn the corner on sweeps and catch the ball for long gains (he averaged 15 yards a reception). He also could kick and punt in a pinch. More then anything, though, he had a nose for the end zone. Johnson finished his career No. 3 on the Irish career list in rushing TDs.

In his senior year (1989), Johnson was named one of the team's captains. He was also an honorable-mention All-America selection that season after helping the Irish to a 12-1 mark and a No. 2 ranking. The previous year, Johnson and the Irish celebrated a national title. Johnson himself had more than that to celebrate. He got married during Notre Dame's championship run—about a week and a half before the Irish completed their title quest with a victory over West Virginia in the Fiesta Bowl.

"I'd love to say it's the most vivid and memorable time in my life," he said. "But it was really a blur. Shelley and I never really did get a chance to take a honeymoon."

Notre Dame had long billed Johnson as one of the nation's most underrated players. Apparently the pro scouts agreed. Nine Irish players were taken in the 1990 draft, with Johnson going first among them, in the second round to the Indianapolis Colts.

Johnson spent four seasons with the Colts, then moved on to the New York Jets, Chicago Bears, Carolina Panthers and finally the Jacksonville Jaguars.

His best season was 1996, when he rushed for 1,120 yards and the Panthers reached the NFC title game in just their second season of existence. It turned out to be the only one of Johnson's 11 pro seasons in which he played on a playoff team.

It was the following year, 1997, that Lane emerged at running back as a rookie free agent and Johnson began moving out of the spotlight. Lane remains Carolina's second all-time leading rusher, while Johnson is third.

"My time in Carolina is the time I'll remember and treasure the most in my pro career," Johnson said. "And pushing football away wasn't easy. In fact, I'm not sure I was smart enough to make that choice. I believe God uses circumstances to let us know. I ended up hurting my back late in the 2000 season. I came back to finish the season, but it got progressively worse in the offseason and still gives me fits every once in a while. But when the wheels starting falling off, I knew it was time to do something else."

Johnson, the father of five kids from ages 16 to seven, dabbled in coaching soccer, selling real estate and serving as a personal trainer before two years of searching and sampling ended up with him taking his current job.

"I'm not sure how long I'll be doing this," Johnson said. "It may look different in two, three, 10 years, but the mission is the same. I see this as giving my whole life for the sake of God's kingdom and sharing Christ with other people and helping them to grow in the understanding of who Christ is.

Part of that process, according to Johnson, is to understand that seemingly bad things do happen to good people—or changed people, like Fred Lane. Part of it is to understand that even someone who is as grounded in his faith as Johnson has doubts and feels his beliefs challenged and shaken.

"The same questions Fred used to ask me, I have asked myself," Johnson said. "I've struggled with who I am and all that. I think in religious circles, they call those times 'crises of the soul.' And I think they're needful. I think they're good.

"I mean, my first couple of years at Notre Dame gave me perspective that I use in my job today. Knowing that I've gone through these things helps me understand where people are and what they're struggling with. Life, to me, is a process, a process of coming to decisions about who we are to God and who He is to us. And that's part of me that will never change."

Where Have You Gone?

THOMAS KRUG

O ne moment Thomas Krug is laughing heartily at the sight of his own dia-per dandies rushing toward the television set, trying to talk to and hug their grandpa, ESPN college basketball analyst Dick Vitale.

The next he is trying to wait out the sharp pains jabbing at his neck, which have nothing to do with the decibel level of his famous father-in-law.

"My neck doesn't go numb, but it's pretty bad sometimes," said Krug, a Notre Dame quarterback in the mid-'90s. "The doctors say eventually I'll have some problems with mobility and things like that. I guess the body shuts down at some point for everybody. I'm careful, but I try not to live my life any differ-ently."

The neck pain has been with Krug since the spring of 1996, when, at the height of his football career, he was told he had to push away his passion forev-er.

Krug suffered a neck sprain in an intrasquad scrimmage on April 20 of that year, a blessing of sorts because upon further examination it was discovered the Los Gatos, California, product had been living with a potentially dangerous con-genital neck condition all along. A jolt to that area, which is somewhat routine for quarterbacks, could mean paralysis or even death.

"I'm shocked that I didn't have any problems with it before then," Krug said. "I had taken some pretty intense hits in high school. I grew up with three broth-ers, and we were pretty rough on each other. But the doctors made it pretty clear. And I didn't just get a second opinion, I got 10. They all said the same thing— given that I was a college football player, I was lucky to be alive."

#11

THOMAS
KRUG

QUARTERBACK

Michael and Susan Bennett/Lighthouse Imaging

Courtesy of Thomas Krug

PLAYING YEARS:
1994-1995

CLAIM TO FAME:
Dick Vitale's son-in-law; stepped into the starting lineup at the end of the 1995 season, helping the Irish gain an Orange Bowl berth

HIGH SCHOOL:
Los Gatos High

HOMETOWN:
Los Gatos, California

PROFESSION:
Assistant prosecutor for the state attorney in Sarasota, Florida

CURRENTLY RESIDES IN:
Bradenton, Florida

Krug, who still had two years of eligibility remaining, credits Notre Dame coach Lou Holtz and Irish starting quarterback Ron Powlus with helping him put his life back together.

"Ron has been a close friend almost since we both set foot on campus," Krug said. "And he was in the room to support me when the doctors gave me the bad news. So was Coach Holtz."

Holtz, in fact, insisted on Krug still being a part of the team and lived up to his word. During the 1996 season, Krug helped coach from the sidelines, threw to receivers during drills and traveled with the team to all road games—including one in Dublin, Ireland.

"When this happened, Coach Holtz was amazing," Krug said. "He became like a second father to me, which I know would shock some people, because even Lou has joked that I might be the guy he yelled at the most in his entire coaching career. But there is so much mutual respect. He cares about you so much beyond being a football player. He was at my wedding. And he knows I would do anything for him."

Holtz's only request of Krug was to try to live happily ever after.

He may be well on his way. Krug's career path has taken him from being a college football player at Notre Dame to the sports business arena to the courtroom. He is currently an assistant prosecutor for the state attorney's office in Sarasota, Florida (they're called district attorneys in most states) with an eye on becoming a judge someday.

"I think why I like it so much is that during a trial in criminal court, it's an absolute battle with the defense attorney," Krug said. "I look at it as who can do a better job of convincing the seven jurors, because in a lot of cases, the facts and the testimony can be argued both ways. It's how you use them to your advantage. To me it's just like playing sports. It's very competitive, so I really get a kick out of it."

For kicks outside of the courtroom, Krug plays golf and tennis and occasionally pickup basketball, although the latter is on the doctor's list of no-nos. Tennis can be painful too if he decides to challenge wife Sherri (Vitale) or sister-in-law Terri Sforzo (Vitale), each a former standout in that sport at Notre Dame. The Krugs, Sforzos and Dick Vitale and wife Lorraine, incidentally, all live within a few blocks of each other in Bradenton.

But the role Krug enjoys most is that of being a father to toddling twins Jake and Connor, who were already playing organized tee ball before their second birthdays and taking tennis lessons before their third. Sherri—who manages her father's business interests, speaking engagements and merchandising—gave birth to the couple's third child in the spring of 2005.

"When Dick Vitale is your grandpa, you certainly get exposed to a lot of things," Krug said. "The twins go to Tampa Bay Buccaneer football games all the time. They go to probably 20-30 Tampa Bay Devil Rays games a year. And they've been to Notre Dame home football games. They already know the fight song.

"I want my kids to do whatever they want to do with their lives, but it just seems like they love sports so much, they always have a ball in their hands. They get the biggest smiles on their faces when they're out there playing. And when they're not playing, they're always talking about playing."

Krug himself was a prodigy in football, and by the time he was a senior at Los Gatos High School, he was one of the most sought-after quarterbacks in the country. But not *the* most sought after. The distinction was shared, by most accounts, by Nebraska prep standout Scott Frost and Pennsylvania prep star Powlus.

Krug was being recruited nationally but was enamored by the Pac-10 schools and vice versa, particularly Stanford. Bill Walsh, the Cardinal's head coach at the time, was a frequent visitor to Los Gatos High—about 20 miles away—for all of Krug's athletic contests.

"You don't want to throw all your cards away, but I was leaning 100 percent that way—until Frost committed there," Krug said. "The recruiting process is pretty weird. I tell people you kind of know who the top 10 guys at your position are. You're all being recruited by the same schools. You're all taking the same trips. You're all in the same magazines. So what happens is when one or two start committing, everything kind of falls into place for the rest of you."

Or falls out of place.

Krug scratched Stanford off his list and began re-evaluating. UCLA, which had a hotshot offensive coordinator named Rick Neuheisel. That was attractive to Krug, but so was Holtz's spiel.

"It almost came down to the flip of the coin—not literally, but it was that close," Krug said. "And when I committed to Notre Dame, my intent was to scare off Ron Powlus and that ND would be my school, and everybody else would go elsewhere."

Powlus committed to Notre Dame at the 11th hour, made it official on signing day and was angling for a shot to be the starting quarterback as a true freshman in the fall of 1993 when he suffered a broken collarbone, which ended his season.

Krug then sat, watched, and learned that season behind the upperclassman tag team of Kevin McDougal and Paul Failla as the Irish fell just short of winning the national championship. It was during the following summer that Krug met and started dating Sherri Vitale.

"I didn't know Dick was her dad at first, but I always liked him growing up," Krug said. "When I did find out, I was kind of nervous. I just was hoping he would like me. It was neat to meet him. It's even neater to have him as a father-in-law. Since Day One, he's been funny, easy to get to know, easy to be with.

Whenever you're with him, he makes you feel like you're the most important person there is."

It was Powlus, though, and not Krug, who rose to the top of the depth chart the next year. Krug did get into eight games in 1994, but his total playing time in those eight games added up to just a little more than 11 minutes.

Little did Krug know Powlus's dominance at quarterback was such a blessing to his own health. At the tail end of the 1995 season, though, it was Powlus's health that was at issue. A broken arm sent the starter to the sidelines in the 10th game of the season. The Irish trailed Navy 17-14 at the time. Krug, who had not attempted a single pass to that point of the season, then came in and rallied Notre Dame to a 35-17 triumph.

That, coupled with a Krug-led 44-14 rout of Air Force the next game, helped the Irish secure a spot in the Orange Bowl. Sixth-ranked Notre Dame fell to No. 8 Florida State, 31-26, in that game, but Krug threw three touchdown passes against the Seminoles.

"When I was playing late in the '95 season, I started getting a lot of publicity," Krug said. "Some articles even said I should play over Ron when his broken arm healed. But you know, that didn't even faze Ron. People don't realize how much he helped me.

"That made the whole experience at the end of '95 even more of a roller coaster of emotions. I had so much fun, but it was too short, too fast. It was just so neat, after practicing for so long, to be able to feel the intensity of a true game as the starting quarterback. But I'll say this too, I enjoyed the grunt work too.

"I think that short stretch in time, being able to touch your dreams, makes the pain in my neck feel not as bad sometimes. That and a wonderful wife and family. I look at them every day and think, 'How can I not consider myself lucky?'"

Where Have You Gone?

MIKE LARKIN

I n between sales calls, Mike Larkin takes in the landscape in and around Oakland, California, and sometimes wonders just what went wrong.

Not in his own life, mind you. Larkin long ago came to terms with his pro football aspirations that crashed in a Buffalo Bills' training camp nearly two decades ago.

"I got thrown around like a rag doll," the former Notre Dame linebacker said with a chuckle. "I was 220 pounds when camp started, which is kind of small for a linebacker to begin with. When I got released, I was 202. It was a whole different world."

He's not troubled by an injury-filled college career either, or the professional swoon his high school coach, Gerry Faust, took at Notre Dame after rising to legendary status in the prep ranks at Cincinnati Moeller.

It's the children that cause the disquieting moments—kids left behind in a now-defunct program called "The Caring Team," with which Larkin was associated for almost a decade.

"It was a very worthwhile program," said Larkin, now living in San Ramon, California, with his wife and two middle school-aged children. "At the height of the program we were able to provide heath care benefits for thousands of children all across the country, children who wouldn't otherwise have had access to that. It was pretty neat to be associated with that. But greed and stupidity ruined it. We tried to resurrect it, but we could never bring it back."

The Caring Team started on a small scale in 1990 with Larkin's younger brother Barry, a star shortstop with the Cincinnati Reds at the time. Mike had just spent two years working for Cintas, a uniform company in his hometown

Courtesy of Steven Navratil

Courtesy of Mike Larkin

#42

MIKE LARKIN

LINEBACKER

PLAYING YEARS:
1981-1982,
1984-1985

CLAIM TO FAME:
One of the three older
Larkin boys who went
on to star in different
sports in college—
brother Barry went on
to shine at Michigan in
baseball and then with
the Cincinnati Reds;
brother Byron was a
basketball standout at
Xavier University. The
brothers were the sub-
ject of a 1985 *Sports
Illustrated* article.

HIGH SCHOOL:
Archbishop Moeller
High

HOMETOWN:
Cincinnati, Ohio

PROFESSION:
Sells pediatric products
for the Ross Products
Division of Abbott
Laboratories

**CURRENTLY RESIDES
IN:**
San Ramon, California

of Cincinnati, and embraced the opportunity to change careers and do something with sports and something to help children.

The way the program worked was that Community Mutual and Blue Cross/Blue Shield in Cincinnati would provide money for health care for needy children based on Barry Larkin's baseball statistics each season. Barry, in turn, would allow the company to use his likeness and would help promote the program. Mike Larkin's role came on the promotional end of things. Under the direction of an advertising executive named Jim Livecchi, the program flourished. Roughly 1,000 kids in the state of Ohio were helped that first year.

The program received such positive feedback that Community Mutual wanted to expand the program to other teams. Catcher Sandy Alomar Jr. of the Cleveland Indians came aboard the next year. Then Crest toothpaste wanted to jump in as a national sponsor, and The Caring Team grew to encompass every major league baseball market.

Then the Major League Baseball Players Association, the union for the baseball players, stuck its foot out.

"They sent us a cease-and-desist letter," Mike Larkin said. "They wanted us to sign a contract with them. They wanted us to guarantee certain dollars to *them*. They wanted to control all the promotions. Well, the public found out this union wasn't what it was all cracked up to be. These guys were scoundrels.

"Here Crest was willing to donate millions of dollars to kids. But the Players Association wanted Crest to give some of that money to the players. When Barry and the other players found out about it, they went to the Players Association and told them, 'We don't want more money. We like the visibility of knowing we're helping kids in our community, doing what we do best—playing baseball.'"

Eventually there was an accord struck, though it was more like an act of tolerance. The MLBPA insisted on having its logo on all promotions and it presented itself as if it were a co-sponsor. What remaining positive momentum The Caring Team was able to retain through that fiasco it lost during the 1994-95 players strike that wiped out postseason play in 1994 and delayed the start of the 1995 season.

"Crest's position was, 'We're not going to spend a million dollars a year to associate with these crybaby millionaires,'" Larkin said. "They just washed their hands of it. Not coincidentally, the advertising agency I was working for lost interest, too. Barry, Jim Livecchi, and I still believed in the concept. We tried to bring it back, but it just never took off. By 1998, it was over."

Soon after, Mike Larkin went to work for the Ross Products Division of Abbott Laboratories. He sells pediatric products—such as Similac baby formula and Pedialyte—to pediatricians and hospitals in the Oakland area. His wife works for Abbott in its TheraSense division, which is involved in glucose monitoring for diabetics.

"Actually, the reason we're in California is because of her," Larkin said. "We were living in the Chicago area, and she got offered this great new job, and I asked to transfer. I'm kind of riding her coat tails."

It was Mike, though, who provided the coat tails for the rest of the Larkin boys growing up in Cincinnati, though all four of them became successes in their own right literally in their own arenas. The three older Larkin boys—Mike, Barry and Byron—were multisport athletes at Cincinnati's Moeller High School, though each ended up specializing in a different sport. *Sports Illustrated* was intrigued enough to do a story on the trio in 1985.

Byron, the youngest of those three, was a basketball star at Xavier University and left as that school's all-time leading scorer. He is currently a financial planner in Cincinnati. Barry, meanwhile, matriculated to Michigan to play baseball before going on to stardom with the Reds. He retired after the 2004 season and has recently gotten involved with Champion Sports complexes, facilities where kids can train for and develop baseball skills.

The most compelling of the Larkin stories may be their youngest brother, Stephen, who was only in middle school when the *SI* article came out.

Stephen followed Barry's path into baseball, but heart trouble would put a crimp in his career. In 1990, he was diagnosed with hypertrophic cardiomypathy. He continued to play with a pacemaker and was still bouncing around the minor leagues until 2004. He did earn a surprise call-up to the majors, though, in 1998. On September 27 of that year, the left-handed-hitting first baseman who had been a sub-.230 hitter at Class AA Chattanooga, joined brother Barry in the Reds infield for one game. He went 1-for-3 at the plate.

Mike sometimes wonders if he should have chosen baseball himself, rather than the football route. Those thoughts didn't surface, though, until he was well into an injury-laden football career at Notre Dame.

While at Moeller, it was almost a storybook existence for Mike Larkin. He was a three-year starter at linebacker, played on unbeaten state championship teams his junior and senior seasons and had college recruiters clotting at his doorstep—except for Notre Dame.

Notre Dame coach Dan Devine's staff didn't recruit Larkin, and he was poised to pick Michigan over Penn State, when Devine retired after the 1980 season and Larkin's high school coach, Faust, replaced him.

"He was probably the biggest reason I ended up at Notre Dame," Larkin said of Faust. "I thought he was a great coach. I thought it would be the same as it was at Moeller, but it wasn't. Everything changed.

"I could tell early in my freshman season there was a lot of dissension on the coaching staff. There were a number of experienced position coaches on the staff at the time. I don't think they felt comfortable taking orders from this high school coach. They weren't 100 percent behind him, and that was a problem. But I think Gerry brought some problems on himself."

Larkin said Faust wanted to focus on developing the whole person, not just the player, but that he was never able to marry that concept with winning football. He, in fact, lost sight of it, according to Larkin.

"Another problem is he wanted to do things that same way we did at Moeller," Larkin said. "He needed to adjust to the age group and to the circumstance. An example of that was that it would be third-and-2, and Coach Faust would be walking up and down the sidelines saying, 'Say Hail Mary. Say Hail Mary.' And I'd have my head down saying 'Hail Mary,' because that's what I was accustomed to in high school. But then I'd hear this whispering out of the side of my head. People were saying, 'What? Say Hail Mary?' It was then I realized that maybe we ought to be doing something else."

Larkin's most productive year at Notre Dame was his sophomore season (1982), when he finished second on the team with 110 tackles. That's more than he had in all his other playing years combined. He sat out the 1983 season after breaking his forearm twice—once during spring drills and once at the end of August, in the exact same location. Knee and ankle injuries in his last two seasons (1984, '85) cut his playing time and effectiveness.

"The knee was the big one," Larkin said. "After that, I lost a lot of my speed, a lot of my explosiveness. I was never the same after that. I guess if I could have seen the future—all the injury problems I was going to have, the fact that I wasn't going to be big enough to play pro football—I would have tried to play baseball. But you know what, my heart was with football then and I always followed my heart.

"And I always will."

Where Have You Gone?

RUSTY LISCH

O ver time, he has become a footnote in Notre Dame football history, a parenthetical statement in quarterback Joe Montana's rise to greatness.

Rusty Lisch was actually more than that. He was the Irish starting quarterback during the 1979 season—after Montana had graduated to begin his storied pro career. And Lisch showed enough snippets of promise in his early days that he found himself ahead of Montana on the depth chart for a time.

It wasn't until Lisch's four children started making names for themselves athletically that the man who was replaced by Montana in game three of Notre Dame's 1977 national title run took a good hard look at how and why it all unfolded the way it did.

"With kids, you always want to strike a balance when it comes to sports," said Lisch, now a project engineer for Memorial Hospital in his hometown of Belleville, Illinois. "If sports become too big and become our God, then we have to say, 'Wait a minute. What the heck is this about? It's a means to an end.' But the balance goes both ways. And throughout my playing career at Notre Dame and in the NFL, I never had it.

"Looking back, I wish I had been more attentive and took more earnest in my tasks, in my vocation. Instead, it was just run-around-and-play time. And of course, that doesn't get it done. Instead of thinking, 'This is where the Lord put me at this time, I'm going to do the best I can always,' I was lax in a lot of ways. I never got to know how good I could really be."

He takes solace in knowing his children aren't making the same mistakes and doesn't mind at all that none of them more than dabbled in football. In fact, all four of them have hoop dreams.

#6

RUSTY LISCH

QUARTERBACK

Courtesy of Notre Dame Sports Information

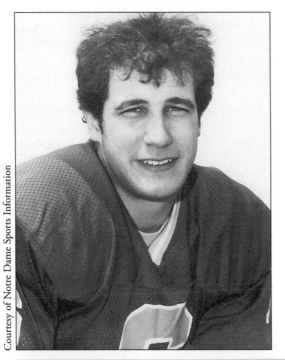

PLAYING YEARS:
1976-1977, 1979

CLAIM TO FAME:
Replaced by Joe
Montana as the No. 1
quarterback in Game 3
of Notre Dame's 1977
national championship
season; came back to
become the starter in
1979 and go on to an
NFL career

HIGH SCHOOL:
Belleville West High

HOMETOWN:
Belleville, Illinois

PROFESSION:
Project manager for
Memorial Hospital in
Belleville, Illinois

**CURRENTLY RESIDES
IN:**
Belleville, Illinois

Courtesy of Rusty Lisch

Oldest child Stephanie entered her junior year at Indiana State University in the fall of 2005 as a star guard for the Sycamores' women's basketball team. She was the first ISU women's player to ever be named Missouri Valley Conference Freshman of the Year.

Son Kevin, the tallest of the Lisch kids at six-foot-two, entered Saint Louis University in the fall of '05 as a freshman guard on the men's basketball team. His senior year at Althoff Catholic in Belleville was truncated by season-ending knee surgery in mid-February, 2005.

Son Daniel, another guard and a high school freshman at the time of Kevin's injury, was the beneficiary of his older brother's absence from the lineup. Meanwhile, daughter Theresa, a senior guard at Althoff, is attracting plenty of attention from the colleges in her own right.

"The kids, my family are such a blessing," said Lisch, a 6-4 forward during his own basketball-playing days. "We do a lot of simple things. We play games around the house—basketball in the driveway, swimming in the back yard. It might sound dull to other people, but we love it. In fact, I treasure it. The troops are kind of dwindling, so we're running out of personnel and running out of time."

Time was never really of the essence during Lisch's five years at Notre Dame (1975-79). Focus and perspective were, and Lisch admits he was lacking in both of them.

He arrived at Notre Dame from Belleville's West High School in the fall of 1975 to find he was one of a gaggle of quarterback hopefuls that numbered in double digits.

"I was really kind of ignorant when I was going through recruiting," Lisch said. "I didn't know who they already had, nor did I care. Then, the first day of practice, we line up for wind sprints by position. And there's like 13 or 14 guys. Montana didn't stick out. I didn't know him from Rick Slager, from Gary Forystek, from anyone else. My only thought was, 'I'm never going to play here,' but that was just from the sheer numbers.

"Eventually, I did notice Joe that season. It was his sophomore year, and he came in and did some exciting things. He had a real poise that would have been real impressive if I had been paying attention."

Montana began to move up the depth chart in 1975, sharing time with Slager until Montana suffered a broken finger late in that season. A separated shoulder sustained during preseason practices of 1976 set Montana back further. Then, when senior Slager went down with a shoulder injury late in 1976, Lisch got his opening.

Some impressive relief work and a strong spring had him running No. 1 going into the 1977 season. Forystek was also ahead of Montana on the depth chart.

"I was kind of distracted when I looked down to the other end of the practice field," Lisch said. "There Joe was, throwing balls—throwing ducks actually. I couldn't figure out at the time why he was putting himself through that coming off that separated shoulder. I couldn't understand why he didn't just quit and go do something else with his life. But there was no question in his mind what he wanted and what he was going to do."

Lisch led the third-ranked Irish to a 19-9 win at No. 7 Pittsburgh to open the '77 season, but Notre Dame fell to unranked Ole Miss at Jackson, Mississippi, the next week and tumbled eight spots in the polls to No. 11. The Irish then faced unranked Purdue on the road and were struggling mightily against the Boilermakers.

Irish head coach Dan Devine replaced Lisch with Forystek, but Purdue's Fred Arrington broke Forystek's collarbone, so Lisch was put back in the game. Then with 11:00 left and Notre Dame trailing 24-14, Devine turned to Montana. The Irish rallied to win that game, 31-24, and plowed through the rest of their schedule, capping the season with a 38-10 rout of No. 1 Texas in the Cotton Bowl. That allowed the Irish to leap four spots to claim the national title.

"When they put Montana in, my pride was still saying, 'Wait a minute. I belong in there.'" Lisch reflected. "Well, as it turns out, they should have replaced me earlier, obviously, looking back at it objectively.

"Even all through my college career, I wasn't seeing things as they were. I was thinking that I should be playing, which I think is good in one way. But in another way, I didn't see the warts that would allow me to get better and to compete. Because of that, I didn't learn from Joe. And probably because of my pride, that flaw carried over into the pros. That really retarded my growth as a quarterback and made me just an athlete who was running around trying to play the position."

Because Lisch was an architecture major—a five-year program at Notre Dame—he was allowed a fifth year without having missed a season due to injury. Irish quarterback coach Ron Toman suggested Lisch be held out in 1978 to have a chance to shine in 1979.

"I'm glad I came back," said Lisch, who attracted perhaps the most attention on campus that school year by winning the MVP award in the renowned campus-wide Bookstore Basketball Tournament in the spring. "But I didn't fully take advantage of my opportunity to come back. To say I understood the game and could read defenses that last year, well not one speck of that happened. A lot of that was my own fault. Maybe somebody could have taken me under their wing, but in college it's such a numbers game.

"Every place is going to have other kids at your position. A lot of it is just perseverance. I look back at Joe Montana, I really think playing quarterback in the pros is what he had made up his mind he was going to do in his life. I didn't make up my mind about anything for a long time. I was more of a guy living day to day, just trying to get through life."

Lisch's athleticism allowed him to stick in the NFL for five pro seasons—four for the then-St. Louis Cardinals before finishing with the Chicago Bears. He played in 30 games as a pro and attempted 115 passes, most of those with the Bears. His career TD-to-interception ratio was one-to-11.

From football, Lisch transitioned into architecture, working for a number of small firms before finding his niche with Memorial Hospital nearly two decades ago.

"I do the drawings and coordinate the design work for the little nickel-and-dime renovations," he said. "Hospitals are kind of known for always rearranging the furniture, so to speak, so there's always little projects going on."

Lisch is proud of his work on those little projects, but he relishes the bigger projects—Stephanie, Kevin, Theresa and Daniel—much more.

"I think I've been able to teach them what it takes to be a winner, by using my own mistakes," Lisch said. "And it's not about winning every time. It's the mental part that separates it. It's the heart. It's the attitude. It's a chance to help my kids be the best they can be."

Where Have You Gone?

KEN MACAFEE

T hey are tucked away out of sight, but never out of mind for Ken MacAfee. The roughly 25 letters came from patients or parents of patients, thanking the former Notre Dame three-time All-America tight end for making a difference in their lives.

They are a persistent reminder to him that life after football has become more meaningful than he ever dreamed, that becoming an oral surgeon isn't necessarily about extracting wisdom teeth, but sometimes about reconstructing faces and rebuilding lives. The letters also reinforce the notion that walking away from his pro football career months before his team, the San Francisco 49ers, won the Super Bowl wasn't all that silly after all.

"You have a little kid who comes in with a devastating injury, and the parents look at them and figure they're going to be disfigured their whole life," said MacAfee, who has settled with his wife and two school-age children in suburban Boston. "So it's very rewarding when you can have a successful surgery with minimal scarring and the patient looks back to where they did before they hit the windshield.

"Getting a thank you is the best thing that can happen to a doctor. That's what you're in it for. You can't be in it for the money, because there isn't any money. You have to deal with insurance companies all the time. The human element is what counts the most, and that's what I find rewarding. And for someone to pause and write to thank you for helping them . . . well, helping people is what it's all about."

MacAfee, whose best statistical season was as a senior on Notre Dame's 1977 national championship squad (54 receptions, 797 yards, six TDs), credits coach-

Courtesy of Notre Dame Sports Information

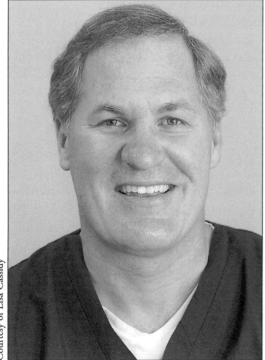

Courtesy of Lisa Cassidy

PLAYING YEARS:
1974-1977

CLAIM TO FAME:
Three-time first-team
All-American, who was
a unanimous choice in
1977; finished third in
the Heisman voting in
'77 and became the
first lineman to win the
Walter Camp Player of
the Year award

HIGH SCHOOL:
Brockton High

HOMETOWN:
Brockton,
Massachusetts

PROFESSION:
Oral surgeon in
Waltham,
Massachusetts

**CURRENTLY RESIDES
IN:**
Suburban Boston

ing legend Bill Walsh, then the 49ers' head coach, for helping nudge him toward his current vocation.

The Brockton, Massachusetts, product had just finished his third professional football season with the San Francisco 49ers, had endured two head coaching changes and a cumulative 6-34 record, and had lived with the haunting thoughts that maybe he should be doing something more consequential with his life.

"What Bill Walsh said to me was, 'You know, you're not quite fast enough to be a tight end, but you'd be the fastest guard in the NFL. I'd really like to switch you over to guard.'" MacAfee recounted. "I pointed out to Bill that we had gone 2-14, 2-14 and 6-10 in my three seasons in the pros, and that although I could see subtle changes coming over the 49ers, that this was a team really going nowhere. So I told him I was going back to finish school."

MacAfee then asked for and received a release from his contract.

"Shows you how smart I am," MacAfee said with a heartfelt laugh. "Hey it's worked out, but retrospectively, it would have been nice to have that [Super Bowl] ring. Then again, who knows the price you would have had to pay to get it. I mean, as a tight end, you kind of run down the field and can avoid getting hit on most plays. As a guard, you're in there mixing it up with guys who are on steroids and who knows what else. To me it just wasn't worth it."

MacAfee came to Notre Dame with visions of being a dentist and not a pro football player anyway, even though his father, Ken Sr., had played pro football six seasons for the New York Giants.

"Everyone always said, 'You're never going to be as good as your old man,'" the younger MacAfee recalled. "And I said, 'That's fine. I'm just trying to have fun. It's a fun game for me.' I never thought I'd be recruited to get a scholarship to college. I never expected anything. It just kind of happened."

MacAfee's arrival at Notre Dame, though, didn't just happen. Then-Irish coach Ara Parseghian blew the Brockton star away with his honesty and integrity, but not before MacAfee got a taste of the recruiting climate in that era. A big taste.

It was a time of unlimited recruiting visits, as opposed to the five-school limit for paid visits these days. And MacAfee scheduled roughly 28 of them to some of the biggest-name schools in the nation.

"After 12, I had had it," he said with a chuckle. "I canceled the rest of them. How was anyone going to beat Notre Dame anyway? Ara was great. He told me about how academics took priority over everything, including football.

"He also made me just two promises—the opportunity to get the best education in America and the opportunity to play for a national championship in football. All these other schools, they'd say, 'We'll give you a Corvette. We'll give you this. We'll give you that.' All that monetary stuff meant nothing. What Ara Parseghian promised me meant the world."

It didn't hurt that MacAfee took his recruiting visit to South Bend the very weekend that the Notre Dame men's basketball team terminated UCLA's storied 88-game winning streak.

"My [recruiting] host was a tight end named Mike Creaney," MacAfee said. "At the end of the game when the students were storming the court, he leaned over to me and said, 'Just multiply this by 10, and you've got a football game.'

"I'm like, 'Geez, where do I sign?'"

One thing Parseghian didn't promise MacAfee was to stay at Notre Dame forever. He shocked the college football world by retiring after the 1974 season, MacAfee's freshman year.

MacAfee was stung.

"My first inclination was, 'Which school should I transfer to?'" he said. "I felt abandoned. Obviously, when I sat down and thought about it, there wasn't a better school to go to."

All three of MacAfee's All-America seasons (1975, '76, '77) came under Parseghian's successor, Dan Devine. That included MacAfee's unexpected run at the Heisman Trophy in 1977, finishing third behind Earl Campbell of Texas and Terry Miller of Oklahoma State.

But MacAfee was never enamored with Devine, who, despite coaching the Irish to the 1977 national title, never did work his way into the same breath with Parseghian in most Irish followers' minds.

"The reason Dan Devine was successful at Notre Dame at all was because he let his assistant coaches do the coaching," MacAfee said. "He was more of a figurehead. I mean every time he attempted to coach, it was not met with very positive results. And he just wasn't very motivating. He didn't have the aura that Ara did. He was a very soft-spoken guy. We really depended upon our assistant coaches to do a lot of the motivating, and they certainly did."

No one has to motivate MacAfee these days. The secret stack of letters and the countless smiles do all the work.

"I'm lucky because I love what I do," he said, "and every day I feel like I make a difference."

DERRICK MAYES

No matter how big the spotlight gets for Derrick Mayes in the coming years in the film and television industry, no matter how many people gawk at his Super Bowl ring, revel at his place in Notre Dame football history, marvel at the sheer splendor of his receptions, the aspect of Derrick Mayes's life that he remains most proud of is a decision.

A decision to return to Notre Dame to experience his senior year after the 1994 football season, when the allure of NFL pomp and pampering beckoned.

"It wasn't about the degree, because I was pretty much finished," said the former Irish All-America wide receiver. "I took advantage of summer school and got done early. No, it was about finishing what I started, enjoying the journey— those ideals my mom and dad and Coach [Lou] Holtz impressed upon me.

"When I saw what that kid Matt Leinart did out in L.A., deciding to stay at USC another year, it was like a breath of fresh air for me. I feel like everybody is so hell-bent on this instant gratification, on this result-oriented mind-set. I think it's perpetuated through the media. I think it's been perpetuated through pop culture, but we're doing a disservice to our youth and ourselves when we go that route. That's not what life is about. I would not trade my senior year for anything."

Nor would he trade his current path for a few more years in the NFL. Mayes played six seasons in the league (1996-2001)—three with the Green Bay Packers, two with Seattle, one with Kansas City.

"I walked away happy and moderately healthy," Mayes said. "I'd rather be the guy to walk out as opposed to being kicked out. I was working in television and film even in my last couple of years in the league. I wanted to be the first ever athlete to produce his own TV show while I was still playing. Eventually I real-

Photo by Don Stacy

Courtesy of Derrick Mayes

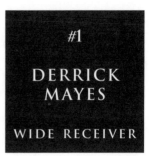

#1

DERRICK MAYES

WIDE RECEIVER

PLAYING YEARS:
1992-1995

CLAIM TO FAME:
All-American who set Notre Dame career records for receiving yardage and touchdown catches

HIGH SCHOOL:
North Central High

HOMETOWN:
Indianapolis

PROFESSION:
Television talk show host, who also has a hand in the film industry and TV sports reporting

CURRENTLY RESIDES IN:
New York City and Los Angeles, California

ized there wasn't enough time in the day to do both, but it also made me realize my passion was leaking out, and I needed to make this transition."

Where that transition has taken him recently is to the point where Mayes became the host of his own syndicated talk show in the spring of 2005. The hope was that the show would gain enough momentum in select markets over the summer that by the time Charlie Weis was kicking off his first season as Notre Dame's football coach, Mayes would have a national following as well.

The show is called *Head Game*. Dr. Mick Franco, a sports psychologist who often works with student-athletes at Notre Dame, is also part of the cast. The producers have connections to *The Oprah Winfrey Show*. Television veteran producer Erni Di Massa has his fingerprints on the project as well. Mayes, himself, retains part ownership of it.

"On most sports talk shows, you talk about Xs and Os, who won and who lost, injuries reports, that kind of stuff," Mayes said. "What we're bringing is an element that we don't care what you scored yesterday. We want to bring a psychological component to the show.

"Say we're talking about steroids in baseball. You can talk about who you assume is taking them and who isn't. But we take it a step further. What provokes an individual to say, 'You know what, I'm going to win at all costs.' There's a psychological mechanism there that says, 'Here's the boundary, are you going to cross it?' Where did you get that behavior from? Was it learned or was it inherent? What brought you to that crossroads and made you take a left instead of a right? That's what we're going to look at."

Mayes said he faced those kinds of pivotal questions many times as an athlete—and even beyond his playing days.

"The one thing I try to curb all the time now is my jock-minded mentality or scholarship mentality," he said. "You're so used to being catered to that you only have to be a one-dimensional person. People tell you, 'Just worry about football. We'll take care of everything else.' You think about how that applies in all sports, in many other pieces of the industry.

"I received the biggest compliment the other day. Someone in this industry actually knew me for my work in it. They didn't even know I played football. I'm proud of my playing days, but I looked it at the way Coach Holtz did: we are not football players. We're people who play football."

Football and TV began to merge early in Mayes's career at Notre Dame. The son of a former high school principal (mom) and business entrepreneur (dad) was pulled into one of NBC's pre-production meetings during his freshman season. NBC holds exclusive rights to televise Notre Dames's home football games. So as the years went on and Mayes's on-field presence grew, the Indianapolis product became a regular presence at the meetings, too.

He also became a star on the field. Mayes finished his college career at the top of the Irish career lists for both receiving yards (2,512) and TD receptions

(22). The two-time Notre Dame MVP (1994-95) ended up fifth in career receptions (129) and set the single-season mark for TD catches (11).

"I knew from those meetings with NBC that I had the capacity to be on-air talent, to be able to talk about football, life, whatever," Mayes said. "I have to give my parents a lot of credit for that. They always felt if you want to play a sport, then you need to take on the role that comes with being the center of attention. You better have enough diligence to speak openly and honestly and intelligently about it."

Mayes ended up going well beyond those goals. He diversified his interests and options beyond football. He started by incorporating himself as a college senior. Then after being drafted in the second round by the Packers in the spring of 1996, he acquired contracts from several universities to produce officially licensed apparel.

While playing pro football, Mayes funded an Internet start-up and a minority-business consulting firm. He obtained his real estate license and created his own real estate development company.

In the last couple of years, though, his opportunities and pursuits have gravitated toward his true passion. He hosted a cable sports show called *Notre Dame Primetime* on CSTV. He's got another show that's being pitched to ESPN executives. And there's a possibility Mayes could soon end up doing some sideline reporting during college football telecasts for one of the networks.

Mayes is also getting into the areas of movie scripts, rights and funding.

"I've gotten this far, in part, because I reached out to Notre Dame alums," Mayes said. "Coach Holtz used to say, 'You can look to the high heavens. You can look as far as the horizon, but nine times out of 10 the resources you need to get ahead in life and succeed are right under your nose.' I used that Notre Dame networking ability."

Mayes and his wife, actress/model Gayle Brown, split time between their homes in New York and Los Angeles, but Mayes makes himself visible all over the country—speaking to school children, making appearances at the College Football Hall of Fame in South Bend, for example.

"I don't look at it as visibility," he said. "I don't need anyone to recognize Derrick's in the building. I take a lot of pride in knowing that I have name recognition more than a face recognition. Maybe that means I have a face for radio, but I'm cool with that if it's true.

"But I do these things, because that's my passion—not for any other motivation. It's an honor to represent the College Football Hall of Fame. It's a privilege to represent my university. I never told my producers this, but I loved coming back to my school so much to do the *Notre Dame Primetime* show, I would have done it for free.

"It's all about the journey and enjoying the ride. You never know what the future holds, but you're never going to know what you could have been if you don't stick it out and assert yourself. If that is your passion, you stick it out and see it to fruition. It can't be about you're not making enough money. It can't be about external circumstances. It's got to be about listening to your heart. That's the best lesson I've ever learned."

KEVIN McDOUGAL

T he spare moments have begun to evaporate as Kevin McDougal's real estate hobby continues to evolve into a career.

But he won't let that free time slip completely away, not when there is a chance he can make a difference with it.

Statistics tell the former Notre Dame quarterback that most of the adolescent boys he talks to while volunteering at The Haven in Boca Raton, Florida, will have futures as troubling as their presents. But that doesn't keep him from praying for them. That doesn't keep him from listening to their heartaches *and* their dreams. That doesn't keep him from coming back again and again and again.

"A lot of people look at these kids, and they can't get past the sad stories, and they kind of give up on them," said McDougal, who has been helping out at the group home for victims of abuse, abandonment or neglect since he pushed away his vagabond professional football career in 2002.

"But there's a lot of good kids out there. They're really trying to get on the right path. You can see how smart they are. You can see so much talent. And, man, you wish these kids had good parents or were in a good situation, because they probably could make it far. And they still can. But you think, man, if their parents only knew how wonderful these kids were, maybe they could have made different choices for themselves, and these kids wouldn't be wards of the state."

McDougal's parents, Walter and Carolyn, knew. The elementary school teachers not only taught Kevin good values, they lived them. And they sacrificed.

They sacrificed so that Kevin's BMX bicycle racing hobby growing up could become so big that he was at one time ranked No. 1 in the world in his age group and traveled worldwide. And they were flexible enough that when football overran that passion, they didn't insist he stay with the BMX racing.

#15

KEVIN McDOUGAL

QUARTERBACK

Michael and Susan Bennett/Lighthouse Imaging

Courtesy of Kevin McDougal

PLAYING YEARS:
1990-1993

CLAIM TO FAME:
Notre Dame's career
and single-season
record-holder in pass
completion percentage

HIGH SCHOOL:
Ely High

HOMETOWN:
Pompano Beach,
Florida

PROFESSION:
Real estate speculator
in South Florida

**CURRENTLY RESIDES
IN:**
Pompano Beach,
Florida

"I have extraordinary parents," said McDougal, who has returned back to his hometown of Pompano Beach, Florida, and lives roughly three miles from his parents. "Since I'm the only child, they're my brother and sister, too—and my best friends. And they've been so supportive. Whenever I've had frustrations in sports—and I've had plenty—they kept encouraging me and telling me to do the best at whatever I did. I probably played pro football longer than I otherwise would have because of them. I stayed at Notre Dame all the times I wanted to transfer because of them. There's no question I'm lucky, and I'm smart enough to know that."

Now if McDougal could only figure out what he wants to do with the rest of his life.

"I started dibbling and dabbling in real estate when I was still playing pro football," McDougal said. "I wasn't sure what I wanted to do when football ended, and I still don't know. I don't have my license and I'm not really knowledgeable about it, but I've surrounded myself with people who are and I love making deals. This could turn into a career. It's taking enough time to be a career—fixing up properties and such. I'm still just not sure what the future holds."

Which is kind of how most of McDougal's life has gone since he graduated from Ely High School in the spring of 1990.

The six-foot-two, 194-pounder had the unfortunate timing of landing at Notre Dame between two of its most prolific passing quarterbacks—Rick Mirer and Ron Powlus.

McDougal, who picked the Irish over Penn State among others, sat behind Mirer for three years, then watched as freshman Powlus wowed the Irish coaches in preseason practices in the fall of 1993, McDougal's senior year.

"This guy was supposed to be the best quarterback to come out of high school in the past 15-20 years," McDougal said. "And then he shows up and he was throwing slant passes for 95-yard touchdowns and screen passes for 80-yard touchdowns. And I was like, 'Oh God, this can't be happening.' I thought I was going to be in a little bit of trouble."

A season-ending injury to Powlus in preseason practice, though, put McDougal and Paul Failla at the top of the depth chart. McDougal did most of the passing and playing in the time-share arrangement. And the numbers he put up were staggering.

He broke Mirer's record for career passing efficiency (154.41) as well as setting new standards for career completion percentage (.622) and single-season completion percentage (.616). More importantly, he helped the Irish position themselves for a national title—all after attempting just 21 passes in his career heading into the 1993 season.

The Irish, ranked No. 7 in the preseason polls and as low as 11th following a lackluster home opening win over Northwestern, finally reached the top spot after the second-to-last game of the season. In what was billed as "The Game of the Century," McDougal and the No. 2 Irish edged eventual Heisman Trophy winner Charlie Ward and No. 1 Florida State, 31-24.

However, an upset loss at home to Boston College (41-39) the next week gave the Seminoles back the inside track to the national title. After a 24-21 victory over No. 7 Texas A&M in the Cotton Bowl, the Irish moved from No. 4 to No. 2, but couldn't overtake Florida State in the final polls.

As disheartening as the turn of events was for the Irish, McDougal could take some solace that when he finally was given an opportunity, he ate it up. Surely, he thought, pro football would be an extension of the 1993 season.

It, in fact, turned out to be a second helping from the past. Pro teams, convinced McDougal's numbers were more the product of Coach Lou Holtz's system than an NFL-caliber arm, declined to draft him.

The then-Los Angeles Rams did invite him to training camp in 1994, but he was cut without ever really seeing any meaningful snaps in practice, let alone games.

"I'm not sure the coaches even knew who I was, even knew my name," McDougal said. "How that happened, I don't know. I was at Notre Dame. I was playing on TV every week. I put up better numbers than some quarterbacks who are in the College Football Hall of Fame. It just seemed like I was behind the 8-ball the whole time."

McDougal tried to get back to the NFL through every conceivable back door—first with the London Monarchs of the World League of American Football (now NFL Europe), then the CFL (Winnipeg Blue Bombers), Arena Football (Milwaukee Mustangs), XFL (Chicago Enforcers) and back to the Arena League (Georgia Force).

He threw for more than 2,600 yards and completed 59 percent of his passes in the traditional leagues (XFL, CFL, WLAF). In arena ball, he was even more proficient—61 percent completion percentage, 7,747 yards, 137 TDs to 31 interceptions.

"Wherever I went, I had to fight for everything," McDougal said. "Whenever things would start to go well, something crazy would happen, like the team would get sold or the whole coaching staff would get fired in the middle of the season. And I'd have to start all over again.

"It finally got to the point where I said to myself, 'I'm 30 years old. I'm not making a lot of money. It's time to find out what I really want to do.' The weird thing was my whole career was kind of like people not believing in me. But I did have someone who believed in me. My parents did. And that's why I can smile now. And that's why I don't want to stop believing in those kids at The Haven."

Yet his days get fuller. His career options pull him in different directions.

I doesn't matter.

"These kids deserve a chance," he said. "Every kid deserves that."

Where Have You Gone?

MIKE McNAIR

The Pacific Ocean lies just a block away from Mike McNair's residence.

His job at C&D Aerospace is more fulfilling then he could have ever imagined. His bonds with his friends and family have never been tighter. It seems like the sun shines every day in every way on the former Notre Dame fullback.

"Hey I just got back from a birthday trip to Vegas," he volunteered. "I kind of lost my voice, but I didn't lose any money. In fact, the blackjack table was pretty good to me."

McNair knows, though, there probably will be darkness to deal with at some point down the road. He also believes he will be able to handle it—because of his support system and because he never ran away from adversity while at Notre Dame.

"I do believe a lot of things happen for a reason and sometimes tough times can be a benefit to you," said McNair, who both lives and works in Huntington Beach, California, these days. "Maybe if I hadn't gone through it at Notre Dame, I would find myself in some tough situations in life and not know how to handle them. I feel like Notre Dame has taught me a lot, and I think it's going to benefit me for the rest of my life."

The adversity for McNair came in the form of multiple chronic injuries and lack of playing time even when he was healthy. His collegiate career statistics read like they belong to a walk-on: 40 yards on 11 carries with a long run of 12 yards, one reception for six yards.

Most players with similar numbers wouldn't even be a footnote in Notre Dame history. But the gargantuan expectations that followed McNair from Corona Del Mar, Califorina, to South Bend, Indiana, and the classy and perse-

Michael and Susan Bennett/Lighthouse Imaging

#47

MIKE McNAIR

FULLBACK

Courtesy of Mike McNair

PLAYING YEARS:
1998-2002

CLAIM TO FAME:
Prep All-American who
persevered through
injuries and coaching
miscues to become a
fan favorite, even with
modest statistics

HIGH SCHOOL
Mater Dei High
(Santa Ana, California)

HOMETOWN:
Corona del Mar,
California

PROFESSION:
Project manager for
C&D Aerospace

**CURRENTLY RESIDES
IN:**
Huntington Beach,
California

vering way in which he dealt with them is what sets him apart to this day. So instead of becoming a player who never lived up to his billing, McNair's legacy is that of a man who transcended it in so many ways.

The (Santa Ana) Mater Dei High School standout was the jewel in a recruiting class that was supposed to help remove any lingering doubts about Irish coach Bob Davie being a suitable successor to coaching legend Lou Holtz. Eleven top 100 recruits dotted the class that signed in February of 1998. That's more than any other class in the post-Holtz era (1997-present) and eight more blue-chippers than the 2004 and '05 recruiting classes combined.

Ironically, the only eventual All-American to emerge from that class was a player Notre Dame and almost every other Div. I-A school shunned coming out of high school. Shane Walton instead came to Notre Dame on a soccer scholarship. He left that team to walk on to the Irish football squad as a cornerback after a promising freshman season on the soccer fields.

Clifford Jefferson, a cornerback from Dallas; Carlos-Pierre Antoine, a linebacker from the Seattle area; and McNair came in with the most recruiting hype in the class. But like so many touted players of the Davie era, not one of them played a down of pro football.

As much as Davie tried to lay the blame on miscalculations by recruiting gurus and analysts, the discrepancy between his highly rated recruiting classes and mortal results on the football field eventually led to his firing in December of 2001. McNair's final and most statistically productive season came in 2002 under coach Tyrone Willingham.

What made McNair, a first-team *USA Today* All-American, so intriguing was that he combined fullback size with tailback speed. In addition to rushing for a school-record 2,671 yards his senior high school season at one of the nation's premier prep programs, he also won a California state title in the 200-meter dash (21.17) seconds and was ranked as one of the top 10 sprinters in the nation in both his junior and senior years.

What's more, McNair's father, Kevin, was a renowned speed training coach who worked with professional athletes all over the country—and his son.

"I definitely knew how lucky I was to have a dad who was so knowledgeable in that area," McNair said. "When I would compete, especially in track, I could notice a serious difference between a kid that had been coached [by a speed coach] and a kid who hadn't been coached. This is going to sound biased, but it's very difficult to find someone as good as my dad at this. It gave me a huge edge."

It was an edge that evaporated quickly at Notre Dame. Davie and his offensive coaching brain trust couldn't make up their minds whether they wanted McNair to be a fullback or tailback. He'd gain weight. He'd lose weight. Ultimately through their indecision, he lost any opportunity of being anything more than a career backup—but he never lost faith in himself.

Nor did he ever lose his poise.

Not once during his career did he lash out publicly about the coaching staff. Not once did he trumpet thoughts about transferring.

"I always felt I was getting better as a football player and learning, even though I wasn't playing," McNair said. "I had such a strong belief that I could persevere through the hard times and find my way onto the field, that I just would never give up and never become bitter about the situation, because I knew I could get through it."

His conviction was strengthened by letters. Dozens and dozens of letters from Notre Dame fans, encouraging him, admiring him. Letters that he has never thrown away.

"I was pretty amazed at first when they started coming in," he said. "When you're in the situation I was in, you're so involved with what you're doing, with what the team is doing and trying to succeed and trying to do the right thing, you never realize how visible everything is.

"I was amazed that what I was doing didn't just affect me and my team, but that basically everyone who was watching was affected by it. That's one of the things that helped me pull through the tougher times."

Another was his friendship with offensive lineman and classmate Sean Mahan.

Mahan lost his father, Michael, to a heart attack a couple of years before he arrived at Notre Dame, then his mother to cancer his collegiate freshman season.

"Sean was stronger than anyone I had ever met," McNair said. "I think that's what made me respect him so much and why we became such good friends. We didn't know how he did it, with so many things going against him. He was an unflappable force and a great friend."

It's the friendships McNair chooses to frame his Notre Dame experience with and an education that helped land him a job as a project manager at C&D Aerospace.

"You don't realize what an advantage that Notre Dame education is until you get out into the real world," McNair said. "There's so many things that come naturally to you that other kids don't get taught. And of course, there are the life lessons, too."

C&D Aerospace manufactures interiors for commercial aircraft—everything from the lavatories and galleys to the bullet-proof doors on the cockpits. McNair's primary focus is working with a group out of New Mexico called Eclipse Aviation Corp.

"They're manufacturing what the industry is calling 'very light jets.'" McNair said. "They're very lightweight jets that are fuel-efficient and have very low operating costs. This could possibly be the future of aerospace.

"It's really exciting. I go to work with a smile on my face every day. Now this isn't what I envisioned doing when I went to college, but it's worked out even better than anything I could have pictured."

As has the rest of his life. He spends his free time at the beach or doing some outrigger canoe paddling. He is also a member of Mater Dei's school board, and on weekends he helps his dad with speed-training clients.

"It's not something I'd want to do for a career, but I enjoy it," McNair said of the speed training. "The biggest reason I do it is that it gives me a chance to hang out with my dad, whose always been like my best friend."

And someone who never pushed McNair to stay home when he was agonizing over his college decision between USC and Notre Dame as a high school senior.

"Man, that was not any easy decision at all," McNair said. "And I didn't realize what a big decision it would turn out to be, which is probably good. But I can say this, it was the correct decision. Every day I am reminded how special Notre Dame is, how special my experience was there, how it changed me for the better—forever."

Where Have You Gone?

COLEY O'BRIEN

C oley O'Brien can recite every one of the warning signs from years of listening to his doctors' caveats, but has yet to experience any of them firsthand.

Roughly four decades after being diagnosed with diabetes, the former Notre
Dame quarterback and folk hero outwardly is the picture of health.

"I think I've been very fortunate that I haven't had any major problems with
the complications that come with diabetes," O'Brien said. "I know at some
point it will take its toll. There are always problems, starting with circulation."

Other complications include heart and blood vessel disease, blindness, kid-
ney failure, foot ulcers, nerve damage, infections and problems that lead to
amputation of the extremities.

"Diabetes alone really pushed me into life after football," O'Brien said. "I
didn't get to chase that pro football dream, but I've stuck with my diet, stayed
active and kept my weight down. I think things have worked out pretty well anyway. I do what I love and love what I do."

O'Brien—a Falls Church, Virginia, resident, husband, and father of three—
does legislative work for NASA in Washington, D.C., these days and has since
1999.

Since graduating from Notre Dame Law School, O'Brien has also been a lob-
byist, a lawyer in private practice, and a cog in the senate campaign committee,
but has never crossed the political line into the realm of public office.

"Maybe if I was from somewhere other than the Washington area, that might
have crossed my mind," he said. "But being from the district, you're kind of in
the middle of that whirlwind, so it doesn't look as appealing as if you were, say,
living in the Midwest."

#3

COLEY O'BRIEN

QUARTERBACK

PLAYING YEARS:
1966-1968

CLAIM TO FAME:
Came off the bench for injured starter Terry Hanratty to help No. 1 Notre Dame play to a 10-10 tie with No. 2 Michigan State in 1966, just weeks after being diagnosed with diabetes

HIGH SCHOOL:
St. John's College High School
(Washington, D.C)

HOMETOWN:
McLean, Virginia

PROFESSION:
Legislative liaison for NASA

CURRENTLY RESIDES IN:
Falls Church, Virginia

He is used to and enjoys life out of the spotlight anyway, although O'Brien came up big during his Notre Dame career when the bright lights did shine on him.

It was O'Brien who stepped in for injured starting quarterback Terry Hanratty on November 19, 1966, during No. 1 Notre Dame's epic 10-10 tie with No. 2 Michigan State at East Lansing, Michigan, and less than a month after the McLean, Virginia, product had been diagnosed with diabetes.

O'Brien's performance that day and in a 51-0 rout at 10th-ranked USC the following week gave the Irish their first national title in 17 years, ending the longest championship drought in school history.

Heading into the Michigan State showdown, the Irish had already lost starting halfback Nick Eddy the day before when he slipped on some metal stairs getting off the train in East Lansing. Eddy grabbed the hand rail to steady himself and tore up his shoulder.

Starting center George Goeddeke was also among the day's casualties, rolling an ankle in the first quarter with a little help from MSU All-America defensive lineman Bubba Smith. It was Smith who knocked Hanratty out of the game in the first quarter as well, driving him into the ground and separating sophomore Hanratty's shoulder on a quarterback draw play.

"I remember [coach] Ara [Parseghian] screaming my name," said O'Brien, then a five-foot-11, 175-pound sophomore. "And I remember not being nervous."

He was physically drained, though, from adjusting to life with diabetes, but buoyed emotionally by the fact that the disease didn't end his career at that point and that he finally got to step into the big moments he dreamed about the previous year as a freshman.

O'Brien originally had wanted to go to the Naval Academy—to play football and to be a pilot—but the Naval captain's son failed an eye test, which made him undesirable as a pilot. Navy was just as lukewarm about O'Brien as a football player, so he set his eyes on Duke, where several football standouts from his St. John's High School team had matriculated.

A chance meeting with Notre Dame head coach Ara Parseghian at a football banquet changed his thinking. Parseghian invited O'Brien out for a visit to campus, but after the visit, the Notre Dame coaches informed O'Brien that they were looking at some other QB prospects, and that they'd "be in touch."

"I figured that was just a brush-off line," O'Brien recalled. "You know, 'Don't call us, we'll call you.'"

Parseghian eventually did call, and O'Brien found himself in competition with three other freshmen signal-callers, including Hanratty, when he arrived in South Bend in the fall of 1965. Although freshmen were ineligible to play varsity football in that era, the thought was that whoever emerged as the No. 1

quarterback among the first-year group that season would be the starter in the fall of 1966.

O'Brien figured Mike Franger was the man to beat. Franger came to Notre Dame from nearby Elkhart, Indiana, as a Parade All-America quarterback and a breathtaking all-around athlete.

"The recruiting ratings weren't as sophisticated then as they are now," O'Brien said, "but Mike Franger was the No. 1 player in the country, no question."

O'Brien did win 10 prep letters at St. John's and did play quarterback and defensive back on two Washington, D.C. Catholic League championship teams, but his résumé didn't compare to Franger's—not even when the Notre Dame publicity department added the claim that O'Brien had once escaped from a rampaging bear to his media guide bio.

"It wasn't exactly that dramatic," O'Brien laughed. "We were not smart campers basically. We had set up our tents at Yosemite National Park in a restricted area. Then we left our food in coolers in our tents instead of in our car. The bear went right in, ripped the tent and helped himself to whatever he wanted. We never actually saw him, but there was some concern that he might come back for seconds, and that we might end up being the seconds."

O'Brien turned out to be a much better quarterback than camper in the fall of 1965, emerging as the favorite to be *the* quarterback of the '66 squad. Hanratty was second, and Bob Belden, of Canton, Ohio, emerged third. Franger staggered in as the fourth option.

"I think if Mike had gone to a Southwest Conference school, he probably would have been an All-American," O'Brien said. "He was a terrific sprint-out quarterback, terrific at running the option, but that didn't fit the [offensive] system we were running at Notre Dame. He probably picked the wrong school for his talent."

Franger eventually left the football team, but not Notre Dame. He switched to basketball and won two letters as a guard. Meanwhile, Hanratty surged past O'Brien in the offseason, enjoyed a strong spring and was named the starter just prior to sixth-ranked Notre Dame's 1966 season opener against Bob Griese and eighth-ranked Purdue.

"I thought I worked hard in the offseason, but Terry evidently worked harder," O'Brien said. "He was taller then me (6-1 to O'Brien at 5-11), and Ara liked that in a quarterback. The battle continued all spring and all summer, but once Terry had the great game against Purdue, there was not going to be anybody to challenge him from that point on.

"I was disappointed. You're happy for the team, but I wanted to play. Fortunately, Ara did get me a lot of playing time as a backup, so I was ready when the Michigan State game rolled around."

O'Brien was so sure he wasn't going to play in the game, he slept soundly for one of the few times in weeks. He finally had gotten the rhythm of the insulin shots down, adjusted to the swings in energy levels and the fear that it might be the beginning of the end of his career.

South Bend physician Dr. Howard Ingle even accompanied O'Brien to Michigan State for the game.

"I often tell him, 'I wonder what my reaction would have been if you told me I could never play football again.'" O'Brien recalled. "It's funny how things happen in life."

To this day, O'Brien embodies the Notre Dame spirit and perseverance as well as any player ever to play for the Irish—even a fellow named Rudy. Instead of sulking over the balance of his career, he reinvented himself. After an audition as a defensive back didn't work out, he surfaced as a halfback and started eight games his senior year. He even threw a touchdown pass to fledgling quarterback Joe Theismann on a halfback option.

Then he walked away from football for good.

"Ara didn't think it would have been a good idea to keep battling the diabetes in the pros," O'Brien said. "And I had some opportunities. But I don't worry about what might have been, because what did become of me is something I'm very happy with.

"And that was made possible by the Notre Dame experience. It's like a family. It's not your blood family, but it becomes a part of you. And it's something that stays with you forever."

Where Have You Gone?

GUS ORNSTEIN

I t was supposed to be a three-hour bus ride to Manchester, New Hampshire, one of the more logistically simple and aesthetically pleasing of the road trips the Albany (New York) Conquest typically takes during its minor-league football season.

Mechanical problems, though, forced the Conquest's bus to the side of the road for four hours and prompted Gus Ornstein to finally reassess if this really was what dreams were supposed to look like.

It's not like the aspiring quarterback hadn't had plenty of opportunities for career introspection prior to that spring day in 2004.

Since graduating from the Fieldston School in the Bronx, New York, in the spring of 1994, Ornstein attended and played football at three colleges (Notre Dame, Michigan State and NCAA Division III football power Rowan) and spent time in training camps and/or rosters of nine different teams in the NFL, NFL Europe, the Canadian Football League and Arena Football2—not to mention a season of minor-league baseball in the New York Yankees' organization.

"The biggest thing for me is that in all of the training camps I had been in, I didn't see a lot of preseason action," said Ornstein, now 30 and a newlywed. "I felt like I hadn't had a chance to fail *or* succeed. I always said if I had gotten in a bunch of preseason games and really played horribly or if the phone had stopped ringing, it would have been easier to walk away."

For now, Ornstein has a least put one foot in what he terms "the real world." He is the director of athletic development at the Parisi Speed School, a conditioning center for athletes in Closter, New Jersey, though he retains an agent in case a trap door to the pro football dream opens again. His most recent venture, though, ended in July 2004 with the Calgary Stampeders of the CFL.

Michael and Susan Bennett/Lighthouse Imaging

Courtesy of Gus Ornstein

#12

GUS ORNSTEIN

QUARTERBACK

PLAYING YEARS:
1994

CLAIM TO FAME:
Thought to be Notre Dame's first Jewish quarterback, Ornstein played football at three different colleges and played minor-league baseball after originally being pegged as Ron Powlus's heir apparent at Notre Dame.

HIGH SCHOOL:
The Fieldston School (Bronx, New York)

HOMETOWN:
Tenafly, New Jersey

PROFESSION:
Director of athletic development at the Parisi Speed School in Closter, New Jersey

CURRENTLY RESIDES IN:
New York City

"I'm very lucky my wife has been completely supportive and had been so long before we were married," Ornstein said of the former Lindsay Stern, a New York real estate broker. "That's not to say it hasn't been hard on her. But she knew this was who I was before we met."

There are times when Ornstein wonders if it would have unfolded more like a storybook and less like a soap opera had he just stayed at Notre Dame.

Ornstein, a Tenafly, New Jersey, product who commuted 20 minutes (if the traffic was good) to high school each day, wasn't fazed at all by the big stage and the scrutiny Notre Dame football players had to live with.

He had been a pseudo-celebrity in his own right during high school. The Madison Square Garden network and NBC had done features on him. Youngsters at the adjacent grammar school and junior high would routinely mob him for autographs. He even made an appearance on *Live with Regis and Kathy Lee.*

And he came from an athletic family. Grandpa Al had been a lacrosse stand-out at Syracuse. Father Steve played two sports at Syracuse—lacrosse and wrestling. Brother Joe played baseball at Rutgers.

Still, there were a multitude of factors that could have dissuaded him from playing at Notre Dame.

When he and his parents took their recruiting visit, the wind chill in South Bend plummeted to minus-63 degrees. Ornstein has already been warned about the weather from rival recruiters at Miami (Florida), Tulane and West Virginia among others. They also not-so-subtly questioned how a Jewish quarterback might fit in at a Catholic institution.

"Everybody made such a big deal out of it," Ornstein said after signing with the Irish in February of 1994. "It's not like I'm going there to break any barriers. I'm not the next Jackie Robinson. I just liked Notre Dame the best."

It became even less of a focal point once he arrived on campus. A local Jewish family contacted Ornstein months before he enrolled and gave him an open invitation to spend the Jewish holidays with them.

"It never became an issue, because the people at Notre Dame made me feel so welcome," Ornstein reflected. "Even sitting at Mass before the games, there were enough guys on the team who weren't Catholic, I never felt alone. It was never a big deal at all."

Quarterback prodigy Ron Powlus's presence on the Irish roster wasn't a big deal—at least not a first. While the six-foot-five, 220-pound Ornstein was considered an intriguing quarterback prospect, Powlus—a year ahead of Ornstein in school—was anointed as nothing less than a savior.

The recruiting hook for Ornstein was that then-Irish coach Lou Holtz planned to redshirt Ornstein as a freshman, and that the Notre Dame coaches expected Powlus to leave for the pros after his junior season.

Due to an injury, Powlus had redshirted during his freshman season. But that still didn't affect Ornstein until late in the 1994 season, when Holtz inserted Ornstein for mop-up duty in a 58-21 rout of Navy. That effectively ended the redshirt season.

"By throwing me in that Navy game, suddenly Ron and I were in the same class," Ornstein said. "They told me that they could redshirt me as a sophomore, but they had broken their promise once. What was to keep them from breaking it again?

"I liked Ron a lot. When I got to school there, he was assigned to be my big brother. We still keep in touch. But I knew there was no way I would get a chance to beat him out. There was no way I was going to sit my whole career and have to bank on him leaving early or getting injured. Had I not played in that [Navy] game, I definitely would have stayed."

Ironically, Powlus stayed at Notre Dame for five years, then struggled to merge his own pro football aspirations with reality before moving into the banking business. He has since returned to Notre Dame as the director of personnel development.

Ornstein, meanwhile, landed at Michigan State, where injuries limited his opportunities. He left MSU in 1997 after being drafted by the New York Yankees in the 20th round, but broke his foot fouling a ball off it during a minor-league game. During Ornstein's recovery, he started dreaming about football again.

He ended his career at Rowan College in Glassboro, New Jersey, and saw his first extensive collegiate playing time there. He led the Profs to the 1998 NCAA Division III title game before falling to Mount Union, 44-24.

Ornstein caught the attention of NFL scouts, but there were more questions than absolutes, so in the spring of 1999, he found himself on pro football's back roads. Ornstein probably wouldn't have been so persistent had he not met and been befriended by quarterback Kurt Warner in Ornstein's first pro camp.

The St. Louis Rams had signed Ornstein as a rookie free agent after the 1999 draft. He was in camp with projected starter Trent Green, highly touted Ohio State product Joe Germaine and the unknown Warner.

Warner had already been on the path Ornstein was just embarking on. He was signed as an undrafted free agent by Green Bay in 1994 and was released that same year. He played three years in the Arena Football League, then a season in NFL Europe before the Rams took a flyer on him. He was even a communications major in college, just like Ornstein.

Had Green not suffered a season-ending injury, Warner may never have gotten a chance. But he went on that 1999 season to lead the Rams to the Super Bowl title, while winning league MVP and Super Bowl MVP honors along the way.

"Kurt's been a good role model for me," said Ornstein, who went back to MSU between football auditions to graduate summa cum laude. "He shows what can happen if you believe in yourself and your dream. I've stayed in touch with him all these years, and he's always encouraged me.

"If this is the end of the dream, at least I can feel good that I never quit. At least I gave it everything I could. That's a great feeling in itself. I'll never have to lie awake at night wondering what might have been."

Where Have You Gone?

STEVE ORSINI

T he notion never seemed absurd to Steve Orsini, but he was smart enough to realize the rest of the world might not see it that way.

The former Notre Dame fullback was only a year and a half into his tenure as athletic director at the University of Central Florida when he was faced with an executive decision that will surely define him in years to come.

Orsini had a head coaching vacancy in football to fill, one that he created when he fired sixth-year coach Mike Kruczek amid a wave of academic scandal and other off-the-field problems, with two games left in the 2003 season and just six months after signing Kruczek to a contract extension.

The co-captain of Notre Dame's 1977 national championship team didn't necessarily need to make a splash with the new head coach, but he needed one who could feed UCF's aspirations of shedding its mid-major image to become one of college football's bullies.

Orsini's thoughts along those lines kept nudging him toward George O'Leary, the man who resigned after five days as head coach of Orsini's alma mater back in December of 2001 because of inaccuracies on his resume.

"We studied it and thought about it a lot," Orsini said. "We even hired a PR firm, because we knew that would be the toughest part of the hire—the public perception, a negative public perception. The firm said, 'Listen, the shelf life of negative opinions of the columnists, etc.—and it will be harsh and it will be nationwide—will be about 72 hours.'"

In reality, the shelf life lasted a bit longer, since O'Leary went 0-11 in his first season at UCF in 2004, but those close to the program did see progress, knowing the extent of the rebuilding that had to be done and seeing that UCF was

Courtesy of Notre Dame Sports Information

UCF Sports Information

PLAYING YEARS:
1975-1977

CLAIM TO FAME:
One of the captains of
the 1977 Irish national
championship squad

HIGH SCHOOL:
Lower Dauphin High

HOMETOWN:
Hummelstown,
Pennsylvania

PROFESSION:
Athletic director at the
University of
Central Florida

**CURRENTLY RESIDES
IN:**
Orlando, Florida

competitive in most of its games. Orsini also remained sold on the hire as did university president John Hitt.

"We had a chance to get a former national coach of the year, and we got him," Orsini said. "We got a coach who Notre Dame had hired. Yes, unfortunately, that didn't last long, but it wasn't because he wasn't a good football coach. I knew George. I knew that he never embellished anything that hurt anyone but himself. He embellished things about himself that were wrong. He admits it. He was contrite about it. He didn't try to cover up and make excuses. He said, 'I made a big, big mistake and paid a huge price.' As you know, the Notre Dame job was his dream job. He said, 'I'll never be able to get over it. I just want another chance to be a successful football coach.'"

Orsini and O'Leary were hardly strangers. Their paths overlapped for three years at Georgia Tech when Orsini was associate athletic director and O'Leary was the Yellow Jackets' head football coach.

"We used to have dinner together all the time, we were friends," Orsini said. "He even took me into his confidence when the Notre Dame offer got serious. And when things fell apart, besides George and his family, I don't think anyone was more crushed than I was. I didn't like to see my alma mater's name get tarnished. I didn't like to see my employer, Georgia Tech, get tarnished. And I didn't like to see my friend, George O'Leary, get tarnished. But in the end, a friend is a friend, and the bottom line is George O'Leary is a great football coach. I think time will bear that out."

Time is the one resource that eludes Orsini himself these days. He carves out time for his nine-year-old daughter, while his wife has even retaken up golf so that the couple can spend some Sunday afternoons together.

"Other than that, I don't have any hobbies right now," he said. "Not that I wouldn't want to."

What Orsini has on his plate at UCF at the present time, some ADs don't even tackle in a lifetime. There's the on-campus football stadium issue. There are facility upgrades or new construction in the works for all 17 of UCF's sports. There's the move out of the split affiliation with the Atlantic Sun and Mid-American conferences and into Conference USA.

"I knew coming in that the president of the university wanted to grow the program into a Top 25 program in every sport we offer," Orsini said. "And yet I came in knowing too, that they didn't have the foundation laid yet to even think about that. But I had the president's support in coming up with a plan, so I think it's fair to say I saw all of this coming."

Most of Orsini's career moves have blindsided him, though, in part because people have pursued him and not the other way around.

After graduating from Notre Dame in the spring of 1978 with a degree in accounting, Orsini delved right into the accounting world, landing at job at Deloitte, Haskins & Sells (now Deloitte & Touche) in New York.

"People told me that I better get my education, because my football skills wouldn't take me very far,' and they were right," said the Irish backup fullback with a laugh. "There were like twice as many rounds to the NFL Draft back then, and I still didn't get drafted. I did have some free agent inquiries—and they were just that—inquiries, not offers. Well, I had offers at all the Big Eight accounting firms, so the choice was an easy one."

Three years after the Hummelstown, Pennsylvania, product left for New York, and just weeks after he had passed his Certified Public Accounting test on the third try, his alma mater beckoned.

Notre Dame wanted him to come back to South Bend to become assistant business manager and ticket manager. The chance to learn under athletic director Gene Corrigan and assistant AD Joe O'Brien was too great to turn down.

From there, it was on to the Dallas Cowboys, where, from 1984 to 1993, Orsini worked for three different owners and moved up the ladder from ticket manager to director of administration.

"Each owner approached the business end of sports very differently," Orsini said. "Jerry Jones, the Cowboys' current owner, for example, cleared everyone out of the front office except for one person, and that one person was me. I wish it was just for my talents, but I think it also had something to do with my salary being lower than what he had projected to pay that position."

Orsini then worked one year as sales controller for Fujitsu-ICL, a computer company that makes grocery store scanners, before jumping back into athletic administration as an assistant AD—first at Navy, then at Georgia Tech, before landing at UCF in the summer of 2002.

Throughout it all, Orsini has never stopped being an avid Irish football fan. He has even more reason to be now, with the hiring of fellow Notre Dame grad, Charlie Weis.

"He's a good friend," Orsini said of Weis. "He lived in my dorm, Flanner Hall, and after football was over and we finally had a life in the spring semester of our senior year, we formed a softball team. Charlie was our third baseman, and we ended up winning the campus championship."

Weis was also player-coach for Flanner's interhall football team, and Orsini and some of the other Irish football players who lived in Flanner would try to catch every one of Weis's games that they could.

"You could just tell he was going to be a coach back then, and a real good one," Orsini said. "Most of the guys in Flanner would ask you questions like, 'What was it like to play Texas?' 'What was it like to play in Dallas?' Charlie would ask you, 'Why were you in Cover-2 on third-and-four?'"

"Charlie was all over it. Even back then, he was a student of the game. I knew he would be a coach and a very good one, but I never dreamed he'd be our coach, Notre Dame's coach. But I'm loving it. That's one of the great things about having been at Notre Dame, following your friends, watching them do well and knowing that you're still as close as you ever were."

Where Have You Gone?

TROY RIDGLEY

There are scars beneath what's left of the wavy locks on the back of Troy Ridgley's head, hidden souvenirs from a motorcycle accident in the spring of 2005 in which the former Notre Dame defensive tackle lost so much blood it required 68 staples and countless prayers to give him yet another chance at life.

"I feel blessed," said Ridgley, who was riding without a helmet and whose head was the first thing to meet the pavement. "A friend was riding behind me in my truck. He wrapped a towel around my head until the ambulance could get there. All he kept thinking was that the crash should have killed me."

That it didn't only gives more fuel to Ridgley's thinking that there really is a purpose, there is a reason that his out-of-control lifestyle while at Notre Dame didn't swallow up every last one of his dreams and every last soul who gave a damn about him. It helped bolster his belief that maybe the sad epitaph so many—including him—once believed was his destiny was now almost a ridiculous thought.

Almost.

"There have been so many times I've been on the road to recovery and then I failed again," he said. "The difference is now I learn from things. This accident was another learning experience—never ride without a helmet, even if there are no laws about it. I'll keep learning every day. I keep doing positive things. I keep talking to kids about the mistakes I've made. I'm far from perfect, but I do have a message. I do have a purpose, and I'm not afraid to talk about it."

Three days after his brand new Harley skidded off U.S. Route 19, hit a storm drain and launched him over the handle bars, the 35-year-old Ridgley was able to walk out of Allegheny General Hospital in Pittsburgh and walk into one of the three Waffle House restaurants he owns in Western Pennsylvania.

Photo by Bill Panzica

Courtesy of Troy Ridgley

#99

TROY RIDGLEY

DEFENSIVE TACKLE

PLAYING YEARS:
1988-1989, 1991

CLAIM TO FAME:
Standout in the 1990 Orange Bowl ambush of No. 1 Colorado, whose star then fell due to problems in the classroom and scrapes with the law; eventually was asked to leave school before his eligibility expired

HIGH SCHOOL:
Ambridge High (Ambridge, Pennsylvania)

HOMETOWN:
Baden, Pennsylvania

PROFESSION:
Owner of three Waffle House restaurants in western Pennsylvania

CURRENTLY RESIDES IN:
Canonsburg, Pennsylvania

On the wall in that restaurant is a plaque that reads "West Penn Waffles."

"That's the name of my company," Ridgley said. "I called it West Penn, because I'm from Western Pennsylvania, and that's where my restaurants are. But it's also the name of the state prison here. I thought it was fitting, because every day when I went to work and saw the plaque, I wanted a reminder of what could have been."

There is a stack of rejection letters from Notre Dame that also serves as a reminder. Ridgley was 12 hours short of his marketing degree when school officials told the former Parade high school All-American from Ambridge, Pennsylvania, that not only were they denying him the opportunity to come back for a fifth year in 1992, but that they never wanted to see him on campus again. Years later, he would repeatedly reapply, offering evidence that he had changed for the better, only to receive the same terse, hostile turndown.

At the time of Ridgley's expulsion, his legal counsel and parents also suggested a permanent move out of South Bend was in order.

"The school had had enough of me. The courts had had enough of me," he said. "I had lied to [Notre Dame coach] Lou Holtz over and over again. My mom and dad had done so much for me, but this was one time there was nothing they could do. It wasn't like you could just pay $200, and you were out of it. It wasn't one of those deals. It was one of those deals where if you continued on the same road you're on, you're not going to make it.

"The courts told me, either you leave South Bend, or you're going to end up staying here longer than you want to. You know what I mean? That's when I hit rock bottom. I remember my dad telling me, 'Maybe you should join the marines.' But I knew I wouldn't make it there. I was like, 'Holy [cow], my life has boiled down to this. I've been blessed with all this talent, all these opportunities, and this is all I have left?' I had setbacks after that, but that was the turning point. That's when things started moving in the right direction. That's when I realized I was at the end of everyone's rope."

Ridgley's four-year blur of intoxication, arrests and wasted potential actually had its roots in high school. The pedestal he was put on as a football and wrestling star at Ambridge High allowed his ego to swell and stunted his maturity.

He could run bar tabs at just about any tavern he wanted—when he was 17. He could be a jerk and get away with it. He could thumb his nose at college recruiters, because so many of them pictured him as more talented than toxic.

"I remember my dad was so impressed by Notre Dame, and he said, 'Do you really think they might let you go there?'" Ridgley recalled. "And I'm like, 'I'm a Parade All-American. I can go wherever the hell I want and do whatever the hell I want.' I mean, I grew up in a town where I could have killed somebody and gotten away with it, because I was a football star."

The allure of Holtz ended up pulling him to Notre Dame, where he was greeted with the culture shock of a web of rules—some antiquated, but enforced to the letter, nevertheless.

Ridgley started out as a linebacker and made cameos in five games during Notre Dame's national championship march in 1988. His star began to rise on the field late in the 1989 season, while playing defensive tackle behind Chris Zorich and Jeff Alm. Ridgley's breakthrough came in the Orange Bowl, where he started and recorded nine tackles in Notre Dame's 21-6 ambush of top-ranked Colorado. Included in that tackle total was Ridgley's smothering of Buffaloes holder Jeff Campbell on the one-yard line on a fake field goal attempt.

But Ridgley's promise quickly receded. Poor grades detoured him to Holy Cross Junior College during the 1990 season. In 1991, he became a starter mid-way through that season after injuries sidelined Bryant Young and Eric Jones. But just weeks after Notre Dame's Sugar Bowl victory over Florida, he began to self-destruct.

Again.

First it was charges of public intoxication and resisting arrest after fighting with a South Bend police officer in a local bar. Then, while on probation, he pleaded guilty to a charge of criminal mischief stemming from his involvement in a property dispute at a home near campus, where he had once lived. Then his grades sagged again. Then he was a memory.

"I can blame it on alcohol, and alcohol was a contributing factor," he said, "But it was all on me. How do you change your lifestyle when all you've ever known is going to parties and chasing girls and having a good time and—by the way—everything's paid for you? There wasn't a bar in South Bend that would take my money. So there was no reason to change. I was happy living that life.

"What I realize now, is that if I had been drafted in the first round of the NFL like everyone once thought I'd be, I'd be dead now. I needed to hit rock bottom. I would have made a [truck]load of money, but I'd be dead."

Instead he bounced around NFL training camps and the World League of American Football (now NFL Europe) from 1993-2000. Along the way he underwent seven knee surgeries and met his wife, Tammy Lowry Ridgley, while he was playing in Scotland and she was a trainer for the WLAF's Barcelona Dragons.

"The motorcycle accident means I'll have surgery number eight," he said. "The other seven were all in trying to chase a dream. You think that's all there is out there, sports and football, because that's all you ever knew. But then you find out you can make money out in the real world, and it's completely legal, too."

It is Tammy who chases the football dream now. She is a linebacker for the Pittsburgh Passion of the National Women's Football Association. The former Troy University softball star, who has a master's degree from Auburn, also works in the Passion's front office.

"She's mean and nasty on the field, just like she is at home," Ridgley said with a laugh. "But she's nowhere near the athlete I was—or the troublemaker. My mom and dad filled her in on a lot of things when we got engaged. They wanted to make sure she knew all about my past, which she already did."

What Tammy also saw was what Troy Ridgley could be. And once Ridgley walked out of his last training camp, she helped him find life after football. And when he was afraid to go back to Western Pennsylvania for fear of what people might think, she gave him the courage to do so anyway. And when Waffle House became a possibility, she encouraged him to dream big.

"I had to work in the company for three years before they'd let me become an owner," he said. "And I had to start at ground zero. Two weeks after retiring from the New Orleans Saints, I was cleaning toilets in a restaurant, but I didn't mind. I knew there was a pot of gold at the end of the rainbow. In the next several years, I'll own 40 of them."

He even finished his degree work, albeit at a school in Florida, since Notre Dame had shut the door.

"I can't blame them after everything I had done," Ridgley said, "But I hope someday they will let me come to a game, let me give money, let me take care of Notre Dame the way they tried to take care of me for all these years. I want to give back so bad. I want to show them how far I've come. I want them to see how much I've learned, that I did make the most of my second chance."

Where Have You Gone?

JIM SANSON

H e had changed his phone number more than once, stopped looking at his e-mails altogether, stopped hoping for a warm smile from someone—anyone—other than his closest friends.

But now the death threats were coming through Jim Sanson's mother back in Scottsdale, Arizona.

For weeks he had tolerated it, figuring it was the seamy side of the spotlight, that most Notre Dame football players had to go through this at one time or another. But this wasn't an unflattering article in the paper or whispers of criticism he overheard walking to and from class. This was something much darker. And so, Sanson thought, maybe it would be better for everyone if he went and started over somewhere else.

"I wasn't ready for this," said Sanson, now living in San Diego and a partner in a sports marketing company called Symbolic Sports Group. "I wasn't ready for the highs. I wasn't ready for the lows. I think dealing with adversity in a very public way is something you take on when you choose to play football at a place like Notre Dame. I just never figured it would take this form."

It was the end of Sanson's sophomore season as Notre Dame's place-kicker, and he had already sent feelers to UCLA and San Diego State. He had made six of nine field goals as a true freshman in 1996, but had slipped to five of 10 in 1997 in his first season under new head coach Bob Davie. Three of those misses in 1997, incidentally, came in a 20-17 loss to . . . none other than USC.

The death threats actually had begun at the tail end of his freshman season when Sanson missed an extra point in what turned out to be Lou Holtz's final game as Irish head coach. A converted PAT would have given the Irish an insurmountable lead with 4:29 left in regulation at archrival USC. That, in turn,

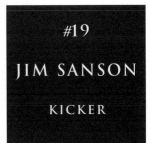

#19

JIM SANSON

KICKER

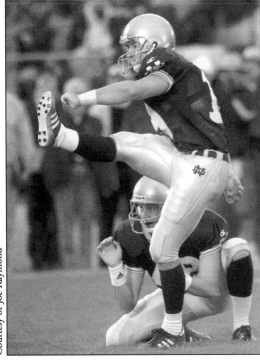

Courtesy of Joe Raymond

Courtesy of Jim Sanson

PLAYING YEARS:
1996-1999

CLAIM TO FAME:
Survived a roller-coaster
career with notable
game-winners and
misses alike

HIGH SCHOOL:
St. Mary's High
(Phoenix, Arizona)

HOMETOWN:
Scottsdale, Arizona

PROFESSION:
Partner in a sports mar-
keting firm called
Symbolic Sports Group

**CURRENTLY RESIDES
IN:**
San Diego, California

would have sent the Irish to one of the four major bowls of the pre-BCS era. Instead, the door was left ajar for a Trojan comeback, and USC finished off Notre Dame in overtime, 27-20. The Irish stayed home for the holidays, missing an $8 million paycheck, among other things.

Quarterback Ron Powlus, who was the holder on the play, tried to take blame, claiming the way he placed the laces on the ball accounted for the kick skidding wide left.

"No one believed him, and they shouldn't have," Sanson said. "But Ron always was great. Sometimes on the road we were roommates. And there's not a better guy to listen to about how to handle tough times and all the stuff that comes with it than Ron. He would put things in perspective for me and brought it all down to earth. That helped me out a lot."

But not enough to make the nightmare stop. Eventually, Sanson sat down with his father, a former linebacker at UTEP and former longtime college football coach, to talk about how to push forward.

The younger Sanson was reminded how whimsical his pull to Notre Dame was in the first place. It started with a cap, a corduroy baseball cap he received as a gift when he was 10 years old. Sanson can't even recall who gave it to him, but it sparked an interest in watching the Irish football team from a distance on television.

That interest continued to get fed at St. Mary's High School, where former Notre Dame quarterback/flanker Steve Belles was an assistant football coach.

"Every time we'd make a big play, we'd get these little stickers on our helmet," Sanson said. "But for me, Steve Belles would put little leprechaun stickers on mine. We were the Knights, but I had all these leprechauns all over my head."

Still, there was plenty of recruiting competition for Sanson, an all-state receiver as a junior and all-state defensive back as a senior. Most of the Mountain West Conference schools recruited him at those positions as did Oregon State, San Diego State, and Hawaii. He also had scholarship offers for baseball from the likes of Arizona State, Stanford and USC. Notre Dame, though, wanted Sanson strictly for football and strictly as a kicker.

"I really didn't mind being a kicker as long as I could play the other positions too, but that wasn't going to happen at Notre Dame," Sanson said. "But it was Notre Dame, this special place that I had put on a pedestal for so long, this magical, wonderful place where everyone felt like family."

The clincher was a letter Sanson's grandfather gave him during the recruiting process.

"I can't remember which coach it was from, but it was from one of the old coaches at Notre Dame," Sanson said. "Back in the day when my grandfather played, they didn't recruit you. They'd send you a letter telling you to show up on this date. If you showed up, you played. If you didn't, it was your fault. But his mom never showed him the letter, not until he was done playing football and was married with kids. He was from Philly, and she didn't want him to leave home. So when he showed me the letter, I thought, well, it would fulfill both of our dreams."

But halfway through Jim Sanson's college career, the Notre Dame experience didn't feel anything like a dream.

"This was not the Notre Dame I heard of, dreamt about," Sanson said. "I didn't make friends with regular students, because I didn't think I could trust them. I mean, back when I was making some big kicks to win games early in my freshman year, everybody was treating me like a hero. Everybody wanted to buy me things. People wanted to buy me dinner. Even though I was underage, people wanted to buy me a keg of beer. I got a million messages on my answering machine, girls calling from all the dorms. I was treated like a king then. Now I was being treated like the plague. I just wasn't ready for it.

"But my dad and I talked. Maybe it was time to *get* ready for it. Maybe it was time to grow up. But most of all, we talked about not letting these people do this to me. I had to be strong. Now nobody wants death threats, but I can honestly say, it's made me the person I am today."

Today Sanson is drenched in perspective and finds humor in almost everything, including his own past.

"My past opens a lot of doors in the business world for me," Sanson said. "They'll usually razz me about a kick I missed, and I say, 'Hey, I hope it didn't cost you any money.' And then we all have a good laugh and move on from there."

Sanson has moved on and around through a variety of jobs since graduating in the spring of 2000. He tried the NFL tryout camp circuit and eventually Arena ball before suffering a torn quadriceps muscle in his kicking leg during a tryout with the Arizona Rattlers.

"I still have a hole in that muscle," Sanson said with a chuckle. "I never had surgery on it. It's kind of a reminder to keep me away from kicking."

His latest move has taken him to the Symbolic Sports Group. The company is primarily involved with putting together hospitality packages for corporations at major sporting events and lining up celebrities for charity events. Sanson has branched out, though, and is working on, among other things, developing recruiting software for college football coaches. He is teaming up in that venture with former Notre Dame football recruiting coordinator Bob Chmiel.

"I'm having a blast. Business is booming," Sanson said. "Everything is moving in a positive direction."

Once Sanson made the decision to return to Notre Dame, his career moved in a positive direction as well—more than he could have ever imagined. But the real magic happened away from the football field.

Sanson did rebound to go 11-of-15 on field goals as a junior, but struggled as a senior and lost his job for a good portion of that 1999 season and even got booed.

"Of course, I wanted to do better, but my whole life kind of turned on a dime," he said. "The death threats became public knowledge, and once they did, the support from the public I received was amazing. The letters, the e-mails, the words of encouragement. It was overwhelming then, and it still is. I got this plaque from an attorney in Chicago named Jim Corboy. I still have it on my office wall, and I look at it every day.

"It's not that I never got criticized again and everything was perfect. What it allowed me to do was experience that spirit of Notre Dame I dreamt about growing up. It put the fire back in me and allowed me to push aside all the crazies and wackos. It showed me there was a true Notre Dame family that I really hadn't tried to be a part of, because I isolated myself so much. Those next two years ended up being the two greatest years of my life."

In almost perfect symmetry, Sanson's replacement, David Miller, blew a field goal against USC in a 1999 matchup Sanson's senior season. The demoted Sanson was still kicking off, though. And his final boot of the game came after Notre Dame had taken the lead with 2:40 left in the game. The ball landed in the arms of returnman extraordinaire R. Jay Soward, who fielded the ball at the goal line.

Soward started over near the right sideline and ran straight upfield, then cut left, just as Oklahoma's Brandon Daniels had done a couple of weeks earlier in returning one 89 yards for a touchdown against the Irish.

Soward, however, couldn't get a block on the corner, so he turned upfield and ran into a swarm of Irish. Cornerback Jason Beckstrom jarred the ball loose in the scrum, and Sanson pounced on it. But he had plenty of company on the bottom of the pile.

"I never had more punches, more kicks, more things grabbed on my body than when I was on the bottom of that pile," Sanson said. "But it was surreal, because I couldn't hear anything. Suddenly, I heard the announcer say my name and the crowd roar. It was almost like everything in my career kind of culminated in that game, in that moment."

The Irish hung on for the 25-24 victory after coming back from a 21-point deficit.

"Our trainer, Jim Russ, grabbed the ball from me as I came off the field and gave it to me in the locker room later," Sanson said. "I don't have anything written on it, but I still have it. I don't think a lot of people will remember that play—they remember the kicks, made and, unfortunately, missed. But to me, that is *the* moment I'll remember. It's about redemption. It's about not giving in or giving up. It's what Notre Dame is all about."

Where Have You Gone?

MATT SARB

T he words never resonated with Matt Sarb as he sat in the hospital room that day, even though he distinctly heard the orthopedic surgeon say that Sarb's shattered ankle—broken in three places—would prevent him from ever playing football again.

He was 15 years old at the time, but already too old and too stubborn to let anything deter him from what he clearly felt was more than a dream. It was his *destiny* to play football at Notre Dame.

It wasn't just that one of his ancestors helped erect the Main Building on the Notre Dame campus in the 1870s or that his great grandparents, Tom and Kate Hickey, once lived next door to legendary Irish coach Knute Rockne and acted as Rockne's sponsors when he converted to Catholicism.

It went beyond the fact that his grandpa, six great uncles, and three of his dad's siblings had gone to school there, his dad had played football there, the now-defunct family (Hickey) construction company had been responsible for 21 buildings and/or additions on campus. This was *his* calling.

"My parents were always supportive of whatever path we wanted to choose," said Sarb, one of six children in his family. "Now, it was easy to be swayed. Our house is full of Notre Dame memorabilia, but not all of us chose Notre Dame. But I knew in my heart it was the right place for me. And no matter what it took, how much grunt work I had to do, I was going to follow my heart."

Today the former walk-on and special teams stalwart for the Irish football team has a better insight into why the grim prognosis from roughly a decade ago never took hold. As a third-year medical student at Nova Southeastern University in Fort Lauderdale, Florida, Sarb understands that his bones were still growing, which accelerated the healing process. He also knows recovering from

#45

MATT SARB

STRONG SAFETY/ SPECIAL TEAMS

PLAYING YEARS:
2000-2001

CLAIM TO FAME:
Walk-on whose father, Pat, was one of the seniors who gave up his jersey in 1975 so that "Rudy" could dress for his final collegiate game; also made a name for himself as a wedge-buster on special teams

HIGH SCHOOL:
Lisle Senior High

HOMETOWN:
Lisle, Illinois

PROFESSION:
Student in medical school at Nova Southeastern University

CURRENTLY RESIDES IN:
Fort Lauderdale, Florida

the tackle on that punt return his sophomore season at Lisle (Illinois) Senior High School and eventually walking in his destiny had more to do, though, with his heart than his ankle.

"I rehabbed and rehabbed and rehabbed and did some extra therapy on my own," Sarb said. "By the spring, I was running track. The next fall, I returned to football."

He was not only as good as new, Sarb was better—but not good enough apparently for Notre Dame to take an interest. In fact, Sarb's only contact from college football coaches was at summer camp, where only a couple of NCAA Division III schools in the Chicago area were willing to throw their recruiting spiel at the standout quarterback/safety in football and state qualifier in the triple jump and the 400-meter relay in track.

"I think a lot of guys at my high school were overlooked," Sarb said. "It was a fairly small high school, so no one really knew about us. I know I could have been a big fish in a small pond, but that wasn't me. I wanted to play at Notre Dame, and I was willing to work my ass off there just to get noticed, just to get my name known."

Sarb wasn't going in blindly. He had a good feel for that obstacles and the heartaches that might await him as a walk-on. His father, Pat, had told him all about the walk-on experience. Pat Sarb, himself, was a scholarship cornerback from 1972-75, whose own career was diluted by injuries. But he had a teammate named Dan Ruettiger, whose walk-on experience at Notre Dame in the mid-'70s would eventually be made into the movie *Rudy*.

The elder Sarb, in fact, was one of four scholarship seniors who gave up their jerseys so that Rudy and three other walk-ons could play in the 1975 home finale against Georgia Tech. The movie script takes license to embellish how that all unfolded, but the message of unselfishness was not lost in the Hollywood-ization.

"I saw it as an injustice that some of the walk-ons, who worked just as hard as me, were not going to get the chance to dress for a game," Pat Sarb said. "In that era, there were 95 scholarships, and only 60 players could dress for home games. Several of us who had played wanted to give these walk-ons the chance to feel the adrenaline rush as they touched the 'Play like a champion today' sign before running out into the tunnel and sprinting out onto the field before a packed stadium for the first time in full uniform."

"It really made my dad happy to do it," Matt Sarb said, "He got to go out and experience a little bit what tailgating was and got to watch the game from the stands with my mom. He said it was great knowing Rudy not only got to dress, but got into the game. My dad had a big smile on his face that day."

That karma boomeranged back to the Sarb family 23 years later. It was the fall of 1998, and Matt Sarb, then a freshman in his first days at Notre Dame, stopped by a friend's place to hang out one evening. The movie *Rudy* was playing in the VCR.

"I don't think you can go through Notre Dame without either having a copy of the movie or your roommate having a copy of the movie," Sarb said. "And as a freshman, everybody watches it. But I could only watch for about two minutes. The emotions and the irony were too strong for me. I was still worried about not making the team. It was *too* real."

Sarb had sent his senior football tapes to coach Bob Davie's office months before, after he had been accepted into Notre Dame as a student. One of the graduate assistant coaches assured Sarb he would be given the opportunity to try out in the fall when he arrived.

So every day at three in the afternoon, when Sarb finished his last class for the day, he'd scoot over to the football offices in the Joyce Center and camp out in the coaches' office lobby.

"I'd stay there 'til five every day for two weeks, just hoping to catch one of the coaches so I could talk to them," Sarb said. "What the secretaries didn't tell me was that the coaches were already out at practice by three. Now I got to know the secretaries real well, and I got a lot of homework done in that time, but I didn't get any closer to the field."

Sarb eventually got in touch with Bob Chmiel, a former recruiting coordinator under Lou Holtz who was then the coordinator of football operations under Davie. That got Sarb his tryout, but no guarantees beyond that.

"Every walk-on goes through the 'Am I ever going to see the field?' question.'" Sarb said. "And it's really difficult, especially for a young walk-on, because the coaches have no idea who you are. They just know you as a number—but even that changes every week, because you're on the scout team (and each week emulating a different player from a different opposing team).

"You spend so much time, too, and after a while, you wonder if it's all for naught. Some guys would keep that negative attitude. Some even walked away, but the walk-ons who really stick together keep you going and keep you focused on your dream, on the fact that this is something you've always wanted to do."

For Sarb, it was people like running back Tim O'Neill, linebacker Mike Zelenka, long snapper John Crowther and kicker/holder Adam Tibble—Sarb's best friend—who helped him hold the dream together.

"If it wasn't for the brotherhood of walk-ons, I don't think anybody would be able to stay unless you have such a high self-determination to play," Sarb said. "There are so many who never get the chance to play. So at the end of the day, you have to tell yourself, 'This is what I want to do. I'm willing to put the time and effort in. This is how I'm going to make it happen.'"

Sarb began settling small goals. He eventually achieved one when he was assigned his own permanent uniform number. It turned out to be No. 45—the same as Rudy.

"I didn't ask for it; it was assigned to me," Sarb said. "I thought it was great in the fact that Rudy really encompassed the walk-on experience at Notre Dame. But I also knew I wanted to forge my own identity, and having that number wasn't going to help."

What did help was the realization that it would be a clearer path to playing by focusing on special teams rather than trying to get on the field as a strong safety. Jerry Rosburg, the special teams coach at the time, took a liking to Sarb and initially put him on the third string of the kickoff team, then watched as Sarb kept working and pushing that subtle opening into a real opportunity.

It finally came in the second game of the 2000 season, Sarb's junior year. The Irish were playing top-ranked Nebraska at home, and Joey Getherall had just returned a punt 83 yards for a touchdown in an eventual 27-24 overtime Irish loss. Courtney Watson, the player in front of Sarb on the kickoff team depth chart, had turned an ankle on the play. Sarb checked to make sure Watson was all right, then took his place as a wedge-buster on the kickoff team. He became a fixture thereafter and finished his career with 13 tackles and two varsity letters.

"My dad was real proud of me, not just for the tackles, but that I worked hard for and achieved something I always wanted to do," said Sarb, whose sister Carolyn is now a member of the Notre Dame rowing team. "That's kind of what Notre Dame is all about. But it's also about family and a sense of belonging. I was calling Notre Dame 'home' within the first week of being there. I still keep in touch with so many people from there."

His demanding schedule at medical school keeps him from following the team as closely as he likes these days, although he tries to keep an eye on the walk-ons.

"I'm in school all day and at the library all night," he said. "I mean, here I am in South Florida, and when I went back for Christmas, I was just as pale as the rest of my family. I really don't ever get to see the light of day."

But at least his dreams did.

Where Have You Gone?

JOHN SCULLY

H e hated those piano lessons, hated sitting up straight, hated keeping his fingers curved, hated the classical music that he was being force-fed.

But most of all eight-year-old John Scully hated that he had no choice in the matter.

"I have a sister and four brothers, and we all had to do it," said Scully, an All-America center on the Notre Dame football team during the coach Dan Devine era.

At some point, though, playing piano did become a choice, then a passion, then a profession for Scully. After walking away from pro football following an 11-year run with the Atlanta Falcons, Scully hooked up with noted Chicago music producer Jim Tullio in the early '90s, and his music career hit fast forward.

"When I was at Notre Dame is when the path started to widen," he said. "I took some theory [classes] and started to develop some writing skills. But it was still very much an avocation at that point. Then when I played pro ball, you have a lot of time between seasons. I knew I wanted to do something with music. I just wasn't sure what. I performed when I was at Notre Dame, when I was with the Falcons and on my own. I decided to try my hand at writing and production and see where it took me."

Throughout the '90s, Scully's work could be heard in the background of commercials for McDonald's, for State Farm Insurance and for Ace Hardware, among others. He wrote jingles. He wrote songs. He arranged. He composed. He produced.

Scully's most widespread success came in 1997 with the release of a 15-track CD titled *Here Come The Irish*. The title track, co-written with Tullio, was used

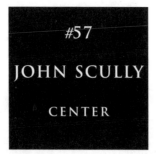

#57

JOHN SCULLY

CENTER

PLAYING YEARS:
1977-1980

CLAIM TO FAME:
Went from a backup tackle to a starter at center and eventually an All-American at the latter position

HIGH SCHOOL:
Holy Family High (South Huntington, New York)

HOMETOWN:
Huntington, New York

PROFESSION:
Midwest Territory director for MSLI, a marketing arm of AIG Insurance; also involved in the music business as a producer and composer

CURRENTLY RESIDES IN:
Joliet, Illinois

Courtesy of Joe Raymond

Courtesy of John Scully

in an adidas commercial and to this day is played during player introductions at various Notre Dame sporting events.

When I remember the leaves a fallin'
And far off music like pipes a callin'
And I remember the golden morning
I saw the long ranks as they were forming

And there's a magic in the sound of their name
Here come the Irish of Notre Dame

Scully, like a lot of song writers, hears a rhythm or a riff or melody in his head, often at times when he's not near a piano or necessarily trying to tap into the creative process.

"One day I was walking up the stairs," he said. "I hear this melody. I went and recorded it and kind of filed it away. A few years later that song provided the basis for Christmas commercials we did for State Farm. It was just something I had in my catalog, but you have to be careful when you hear those melodies in your head. You think you're a genius one day, and then the next day you realize the Beatles wrote that."

Eventually the noises in his head told Scully it was time to scale the music back to a part-time venture. In 2001, he got into the insurance business. He is currently the Midwest Territory Director for MSLI, a marketing arm for AIG Insurance.

"When somebody first suggested I go into the insurance business, I thought they were crazy," Scully said. "But what I do is actually the people side of the business. And I like that, because it's all about relationships."

Scully's relationship with music, which is still alive on weekends during slow spots in his schedule, almost altered his football career. The Huntington, New York, product became fascinated with Penn State, in part because of its renowned music department, and in part because Mike Reid played football and honed his fledgling music career there.

Today Reid, a pianist like Scully, is one of the hottest song writers in country music, penning songs for some of that genre's biggest stars. He has a Grammy to his credit—and an Outland Trophy from his days at Penn State before starring as a defensive lineman for the Cincinnati Bengals.

"He was part of Penn State's recruiting film, and I was very impressed with the guy," Scully said. "I'm still a big fan of his. One of my favorite songs is one he wrote for Bonnie Raitt—'I Can't Make You Love Me.' But in the end, I chose Notre Dame. I thought it was just better for national recognition."

After arriving at Notre Dame, though, Scully began to doubt whether there'd even be modest recognition—at least where football was concerned. He missed his freshman season (1976) with an injury, and only played sparingly as a reserve tackle on the 1977 national championship squad the next year. He still was a backup heading into the 1979 season, when All-America center Dave Huffman's graduation opened up a spot on the line.

Scully had played some center early in his high school career and decided to give it a shot. He became the starter that year and earned consensus All-America honors as a fifth-year senior in 1980.

"The thing I remember most about my time at Notre Dame was that it was not easy, the football part of it, that is," Scully said. "Football just didn't come as easily to me as it did for other people. I guess it just goes to show that if you keep showing up for work every day, and if you make an impression over a period of time, sometimes you get your chance. That kind of stuff looks a lot better in the rear-view mirror than it looks dead ahead in the road. I wouldn't want to relive every hurdle I had to jump, but in retrospect it was good for me."

Along the way, Scully became friends with Tom Thayer and his family. Thayer was a standout offensive guard at Notre Dame out of Joliet (Illinois) Catholic, the same high school that produced walk-on wonder Rudy several years prior. Thayer's family routinely made the short trip over to South Bend, which is how Scully met Thayer's sister, Annette—now Annette Scully.

After Scully's pro career was over, the couple moved from Atlanta to Joliet, which remains their home today. The couple's teenage daughters, Britt and Annie, are students at Rudy's alma mater, Joliet Catholic. They share their dad's passion for music, having lent their voices as backup singers to one of Scully's commercial productions.

"My wife is very supportive of the music," Scully said, "and she is the one who holds everything together. She simplifies our lives. She takes care of the house from top to bottom. She works out at five in the morning every day for a couple of hours. All the rest of us find our instructions for the day by our cereal bowls."

Scully would like to say it was family that prompted him to push away pro football and gravitate toward music. Actually, the extra family time was just a fringe benefit. The resurfacing of an old injury prompted the fourth-round draft choice to retire after playing center for the Falcons from 1981 to 1991.

"I had broken my leg in half in 1985 in Dallas, three weeks before Joe Theismann did the same thing," Scully said. "Well in 1991, they told me they were going to have to saw it in half and reset it if I kept playing. So I thought, 'Yeah, this is a good time to move on with life.'

"It's funny, because when I first got drafted, I was hoping I could just make the team for a year so I could put it on my résumé. I had no idea it would last, especially since there was a knock on me that I wasn't big and mean enough in the beginning. I guess you sink or swim. I know I learned a lot, and the most important lesson I learned is that it's not about the winning or having a championship ring or playing in the Super Bowl. The true value is you learn that you *don't* win 'em all, that there's always a reason to get up in the morning and try again."

Scully can't remember the exact day or even the year he woke up, and taking piano lessons was fun for the first time. He does know that he is glad it happened. He's also pretty proud of his old piano teacher, Marga Richter, who went on to become a famous composer.

"All of the kids in my family still carry some of that music with us into today," Scully said. "Maybe it's just singing in the church choir on weekends, like my brother, the cardiologist, does. But it's still there. It's the best thing that could have happened to ground us. I guess my parents knew what they were doing."

Where Have You Gone?

AARON TAYLOR

There is a child crying, sobbing inconsolably somewhere in Kosgoda, Sri Lanka. Her mother was too far back in the food line when the truck teeming with strangers and goodwill ran out of the latter. As the truck pulls away, the mother chases it, pleading, weeping until exhaustion takes her breath and legs away.

There is a beggar with a cup on the streets of Kosgoda, a coastal community whose picturesque palm trees dancing in the wind belie the heartache and devastation around them. The beggar is shaking his cup, hoping the sound of the coins rattling will transform the sympathetic passersby into human ATMs.

Even the savviest of the volunteers, in Sri Lanka because of their oversized hearts and supercharged drives, struggle with this picture. They know that some of the beleaguered souls standing on the corners have no other means to survive another day. But some will buy drugs with the money. And there are still others, dropped off by the busload in the capital city of Colombo, who pose and panhandle to support the projects and corruption of the underworld.

There is a homeless woman dying in Kosgoda just before a makeshift home—12 feet by 18 feet with a wooden exterior, steel roof and a floor made from concrete—promised to her is completed. Word is she suffered a heart attack when rumor of a second tsunami gripped her with such terror, her body couldn't contain it. An earthquake did shake the island of Sumatra, Indonesia, on March 29, 2005, but there were no giant waves to follow this time.

Outside of the dead women's unfinished home, a small group of people squabble over which of them deserves to move in now. An American man, whose only mastered phrases in the Sinhala language are: "I'm hungry," and "That girl is pretty," is left to make the decision who stays homeless and who does not.

#75

AARON
TAYLOR

OFFENSIVE
TACKLE /
OFFENSIVE
GUARD

PLAYING YEARS:
1990-1993

CLAIM TO FAME:
Unanimous first-team
All-America tackle in
1993 after earning con-
sensus All-America
honors at offensive
guard the previous year;
also won the Lombardi
Award in '93

HIGH SCHOOL:
De La Salle High

HOMETOWN:
Concord, California

PROFESSION:
College football studio
analyst for ABC-TV

**CURRENTLY RESIDES
IN:**
San Diego, California
and New York City

These are the images that chase Aaron Taylor, a 290-pound bundle of mixed emotions, on April 5, 2005, as Qatar Airways Flight 303 taxis down the lone runway at Bandaranaike International Airport, just north of Colombo.

"I know for sure I did some good. I do not question that whatsoever," said Taylor, a former All-America offensive lineman at Notre Dame in the early '90s who spent thousands of dollars of his own money to finance two trips to Sri Lanka in early 2005 with the sole purpose of making a difference.

"But the overwhelming emotion I felt upon leaving Sri Lanka was frustration," he said. "It was extremely difficult, more difficult than I assumed it was going to be, and I think unnecessarily so. I was working so much harder than most of the people I was trying to help and certainly harder than their own government was willing to work for them. For many days, I questioned what the heck I was doing there.

"I came to find out that much of the apathy—kind of sitting back with your arms folded and letting other people do things for you—is ingrained in their culture from centuries of colonialism. First the Portuguese, then the Dutch, then the English came in. Over time these people became willing to follow anybody and let them take control as long as they get thrown little biscuits. So, here I sit once again, desperately sniffing my psyche for the faint aroma of some divine experience I feel owed to me."

There is a family waiting for Taylor to come home to them, to share every snapshot, every detail in person, even though they've followed it all along through e-mails and crackly long-distance phone calls at odd hours of the night.

Michael Schafer, an engineering professor at Notre Dame, is a man Taylor met by chance 15 years earlier when his freshman-year roommate, Eric Griggs, dragged him and Notre Dame tight end Oscar McBride along to the Schafers' Granger, Indiana, home with only the promise of a home-cooked meal.

Over time Taylor became, first, an oversized smiling face, then a baby-sitter, then a big brother to Mike and Katie's three children—Bobby, John, and Ann. And Mike and Katie became, first, parents, then so much more.

"Very quickly I realized their interest in me was much greater than having a Notre Dame football player over to their house," said Taylor, whose mom was 2,000 miles away in California and whose father was never in the picture. "In fact, it had nothing to do with that. What I love about their family is that from very early on, they let me be me. I never had to be number 75 or a left tackle or a Golden Domer.

"In turn, I held those kids as babies, and I've watched them grow up and take part in so many things. They've been a tremendous source of love and support. They are my family."

And they continued to be so when Taylor became a first-round draft choice of the Green Bay Packers in the spring of 1994 and when he won a Super Bowl with that team in January of 1997. But they were also there when a torn patellar tendon in his right knee wiped out his entire rookie season and when an almost identical injury in his left knee, suffered in the playoffs the following season, necessitated another surgery.

They came to understand and expect his life changes that looked like disjointed left turns to the rest of the world, but had a rhythm and connection in theirs and Taylor's eyes. Like went he retired from pro football after six seasons, leaving half of his four-year, $10.8-million contract with the San Diego Chargers on the table.

"I could have sucked it up for another year," Taylor said, "but I was in so much pain and taking so many pills and so many shots and so many drugs to play at a level that was well below my comfort level. I would imagine it was certainly below the team's comfort level. The more I did, the less I was able to produce, and I was miserable. There are more important things in life than money, such as my health and happiness, and so I walked."

Walked away from football and toward a career as an elementary school teacher, that would have seemed absurd to Taylor weeks before it manifested, but now it felt like destiny.

"A buddy of mine's sister was a fourth-grade teacher, and I asked if I could go by her class," Taylor said. "I was there only 15 minutes and the light bulb exploded. 'Oh my God,' I thought. 'This is perfect.'"

Then another door opened up with ABC-TV. Taylor was a student teacher for a class of second-graders in San Diego when he went for an audition. He was officially named a college football studio analyst for the network a few weeks later, in July of 2004.

"ABC was opportunistic," he said. "Teaching is what I want to do. When I'm 60 years old, I would hope I would have taught. I still think about it, still long to do it. I'm also realizing there are other ways to teach that don't necessarily have to be in a classroom dynamic. But I'm having fun right now, and I really enjoy what I do with ABC. It provides me some opportunities to do some other wonderful things, like Sri Lanka."

Taylor was actually headed to New Zealand for a pleasure trip when he saw the horrifying images on TV the day after Christmas 2004. He saw the Indian Ocean swallowing up Sri Lanka, an island nation sadly, fittingly, shaped like a teardrop. Up until that moment he couldn't have found Sri Lanka, a country about the size of West Virginia on a globe with roughly 10 times as many people (20 million). He had to do a Google search on the Internet to locate it, learn about this land where more than 40,000 were killed in that nation and 850,000 left homeless in one, senseless, inexplicable act of nature.

It was no surprise to the Schafers when Taylor abruptly changed his travel plans to change someone else's life. "Why is the sky blue?," they figured. "Why does the Earth spin? Because that's who Aaron Taylor is."

Wrote Taylor to the Schafers upon leaving for Sri Lanka in late January: "Cataclysmic events such as these—9/11 for many of us—oftentimes serve as a catalyst for reflective thinking. And the incident on 12/26 helped to further my own ongoing realization that I have been particularly blessed in life. Consequently, I am choosing to travel to a faraway place to help strangers to physically and emotionally rebuild their lives—not because I *have* to, but because I am *able* to."

Before Taylor left Asia, soaked in sweat and overwhelm, he had helped build temporary homes for 40 families.

There is a mother smiling in the Bay Area, not only because her son changed his own troubled life, but also because he has touched so many other lives so positively since.

Mardi Taylor worked as a pediatric nurse in California's Bay Area, but struggled to be both a mother and father to Aaron after splitting with her husband when Aaron was a toddler. The family moved frequently, sometimes because of a new job, sometimes because the house they were renting was about to be sold, but wherever they landed, Taylor found trouble.

"For the most part, I was falling into peer pressure," Taylor said. "Maybe it was hard for me [to move so much] and the way I chose to adapt, to fit in, was to do drugs, to party and to not do well in school. Those aren't things that healthy, happy kids take part in."

Nor is stealing a motorcycle when you're 14 years old and riding it across the Richmond Bridge at 120 miles an hour in the rain.

"The turning point was a combination of things," Taylor said. "There was always a feeling inside of me that I could do more. I realized on some level that I was selling out and that I was going down a road that was beneath me, that I was lowering the bar.

"I don't know where I got that from. Maybe I was born with it, but my mother certainly fostered a lot of that, specifically with a conversation we had where she just kind of walked me through choices and consequences. That's when the light bulb finally went on, that I was going to be left with very few choices if I continued down the road I was on. She helped me think about goals and opportunities. I very much appreciate and respect her more and more each day for what she did to help create the opportunity, which was to play football."

Taylor wasn't exactly sure why he gravitated to football at that point. He was going into his junior year in high school and had logged just one season of organized football, that at Mount Tamalpais High School in Mill Valley, California. By his own admission, Taylor wasn't very good at the sport and really didn't enjoy it all that much.

"The serendipitous aspect of the story," Taylor said. "is that it was almost like once I determined what I wanted to do, the universe kind of opened up, and God was like, 'OK, here you go.'"

In the weeks that followed, Taylor saw a program on TV about a perennial high school football power across the bay in Concord called De La Salle High School. Then a job opened up for his mom in that area, a nice place with very affordable rent one mile down the road became available, and Taylor was in. The only struggle was paying the tuition, which Taylor helped out with.

"It about broke us," he said. "I worked, picked up trash, did whatever I had to do. And my mom did whatever she had to do."

Taylor's football potential swelled into prowess at De La Salle. Even with limited experience, he attracted recruiting attention from coast to coast. Tom Bowen, the athletic director at De La Salle at the time and a Notre Dame grad, kept dropping not-so-subtle hints to Taylor about Notre Dame.

"I didn't even know where Notre Dame was at first," Taylor said. "I thought it was in England somewhere. Every day he'd talk to me about it. Eventually I decided on five recruiting trips—four Pac-10 schools and Notre Dame. Well it was my first recruiting trip, and when I got off the plane in South Bend, it just felt right."

Taylor went on to become one of the most dominant offensive linemen in Irish history. After winning consensus All-America honors as a junior at left guard in 1992, he shifted over to left tackle in '93 and was a *unanimous* All-American there. He also took home the Lombardi Trophy, emblematic of the nation's top lineman on either side of the ball.

"Something resonated with me right away with what Notre Dame was about," he said. "No names on the backs of the jerseys. The team is more important than the individual. It's a Catholic university. It's a concept of teamwork. All those sorts of things that were instilled in me at De La Salle were also at Notre Dame."

There is a dream sowing somewhere inside Aaron Taylor. Amidst the disillusion and frustration rattling around in Taylor's head, there is still hope, still ideas, still drive.

"Before I left for Sri Lanka, I knew that when I came back, I wanted to do something to help the people in this country, the U.S.," Taylor said. "I still have that burning desire. Now how I do that may have changed. I've seen with my own eyes and experienced dynamics where I think I've flushed out my feelings on whether you give a man a fish or teach a man to fish.

"I think sometimes going in with good intentions and wanting to help people and doing things for them isn't necessarily in their best interests or yours. I don't know if I ever felt that way before. I'm going to take some time to let this thing settle out, because I don't want to make emotional decisions. But I'm going to find a way help and do it right. I'm going to find a way to make it work, not because I have to, but because I can."

And in that vision, somewhere there will be one less child crying.

As Taylor's thoughts come back to the present time, he settles into seat 11A and fastens his seat belt. The engines rumble and the plane lifts into the sky, and Aaron Taylor's spirits soar.

Where Have You Gone?

PAT TERRELL

P at Terrell tottered toward the TV set, still groggy from being aroused earlier than expected on his day off.

His wife, Beth, pointed toward the images flickering on the TV, replays of an airplane inexplicably crashing into the World Trade Center's north tower in New York City.

"I just thought, 'My goodness, it's a clear day. What in the world?'" recalled Terrell, a former All-America safety at Notre Dame who had become a professional pilot in 1999 following a nine-year run in the NFL.

"At the time we didn't know if it was a big plane, a small plane," Terrell continued. "My first thought was that at that time you were able to rent a small plane and fly around Manhattan. So I thought maybe it was just an inexperienced pilot. Then the second plane hit, and I was just utterly confused. The thought that this was terrorism never entered my mind until they mentioned it on TV."

Eventually, Terrell would learn that the first plane to hit on September 11, 2001 was American Airlines Flight 11 out of Boston's Logan Airport, the same airport Terrell had flown out of the day before as a commercial airline pilot.

"I almost got out of the industry right after that," said Terrell, the father of five children all under the age of seven. "I never lost my love and desire to fly, but it certainly damaged the careers of pilots and crippled the industry. I was thinking about turning it back into a hobby instead of a career, but I didn't. And I'm glad I didn't."

In the weeks that followed the 9/11 tragedies, Terrell—who now flies 757s and 767s for ATA Airlines and lives in the Chicago area—came up with a little preflight ritual that became a mental security blanket for him.

Br. Charles McBride, C.S.C.

Courtesy of Pat Terrell

PLAYING YEARS:
1986-1989

CLAIM TO FAME:
Knocked away Miami's
two-point conversion
attempt in the closing
moments of a 31-30
Irish upset of the top-
ranked Hurricanes that
ultimately led to Notre
Dame capturing the
1988 national champi-
onship

HIGH SCHOOL:
Lakewood High

HOMETOWN:
St. Petersburg, Florida

PROFESSION:
Commercial airline
pilot for ATA Airlines;
also owns a develop-
ment company in
Chicago—The Terrell
Group

**CURRENTLY RESIDES
IN:**
Hinsdale, Illinois

"I was still in pretty good football shape," he said, "so prior to every flight, I'd kind of roll my sleeves up and stick my chest out a little bit and walk up and down the aisle, just to let any crazy guys who might be on the plane know that if they think they're going to come up to the cockpit and find a little nervous guy sitting there, then they'd have something else coming."

On one particular flight, though, Terrell was late getting to the plane and didn't have time to go through the whole ritual, so he opened the cockpit door and sort of stared down the passengers as they boarded the plane.

"All of a sudden, I see this guy's head lean out into the middle of the aisle," Terrell said. "And this particular individual's eyes grew the size of golf balls. Sure enough, it was Tony Rice."

Rice was the quarterback on Notre Dame's 1988 national championship team. Terrell was a free safety on that squad who was best known for swatting away a two-point conversion attempt in '88 against No. 1 Miami. The deflection, which came with 45 seconds left in the game, secured the 31-30 Irish upset and gave fourth-ranked Notre Dame the momentum to eventually move into the No. 1 spot for good three weeks later.

"Tony thought I was still playing football for Green Bay," Terrell recalled of their chance meeting aboard the airplane. "I'm sure the first thought in his mind was, 'What is this, Halloween?' I must have laughed about it for three days."

Most of Terrell's Notre Dame teammates knew of his passion for flying. "The scared fliers would usually sit next to me to ask, 'What was that?' every time they heard a noise or we'd hit an air pocket," Terrell said.

What they didn't know was how much he wanted to turn it into a career. He was a marketing major at Notre Dame.

Some of his choice of majors had to do with Terrell wanting to diversify post-football options, but some of it was some unintentional deception on Irish head football coach Lou Holtz's part during the recruiting process.

Terrell, an all-state quarterback and safety in talent-rich Florida, was looking seriously at the Air Force Academy, Georgia Tech and Purdue for their engineering and aviation expertise. Holtz, initially unaware of Terrell's aviation ambitions, was curious why an athlete the caliber of the St. Petersburg Lakewood High product would so readily shun Miami, for instance, and put together such an odd assortment of schools, odd at least when looking through the eyes of a football coach.

"I told him it was because of their aviation backgrounds," Terrell said. "His response to that was, 'Well we've got an airport right here in South Bend.' Unfortunately, I didn't see that airport except for charter flights to go play games. It was kind of our ongoing little joke."

Once at Notre Dame, Terrell was led to believe he would play receiver, a position in which he dabbled at Lakewood High. He was looking forward to the conversion when Holtz swiftly and decisively switched him to cornerback instead in the fall of 1986.

"Even though I had played some safety in high school, I never thought of myself as a defensive player," Terrell said. "But they had a need, and it was a way to get on the field early. All I asked was that they'd promise me they'd move me back to receiver the next year."

Wish granted. But it wasn't at all how Terrell has envisioned it. By midseason he was starting opposite eventual '87 Heisman Trophy winner Tim Brown. But heading into the Cotton Bowl, he had just two catches for the season.

"That's a pretty embarrassing statistic when you're a receiver," he said.

The beginning of the end of his days on offense unfolded at a practice leading up to the Cotton Bowl. Thousands of Irish fans, including Terrell's parents, had come to watch the Irish practice in Dallas.

Terrell was having a particularly tough day when, near the end of practice, Rice called a play that required Terrell to catch the ball over the middle of the field on a crossing route.

"Our practices, at times, were so much more intense than the games," Terrell said. "Players would actually look forward to the games, because they were easier, especially on the offensive side of the ball, because that's where Holtz was. And this was one of those days.

"Well Tony Rice throws this absolutely beautiful ball that hits me right in the chest, and I drop it. Well, I had been with Holtz all season. I knew what was coming."

Or so he thought. Holtz, who had been standing beyond the safeties, came running full speed at Terrell, but then ran right past him, past the linebackers, through the offensive line and stopped inches away from Rice's face.

"He's yelling at Tony, 'I don't care how open Pat Terrell is.'" Terrell recounted. "'I don't care if you can walk up and hand him the football. Do not throw the ball to Pat Terrell. Take the sack.'

"Now I'm standing there, and I've been a fighter all my life. My parents taught me not to quit anything, but for the first time in my life, it was crossing my mind. I can't take this. Then he blows the whistle, practice is over and I think he's coming over to me to apologize. He puts his arm around me and says, 'Son, you're one of the best receivers I've ever coached—until we throw you the football. We're moving you to free safety next year.'"

Terrell was slow to warm up to the move and initially shared time at the position with Corny Southall in 1988. The Miami game in mid-October was just his second start of the season.

Hurricanes quarterback Steve Walsh ended up having his most prolific day as a collegiate quarterback against the Irish, but turnovers and big defensive plays allowed Notre Dame to snap Miami's 36-game regular-season win streak anyway.

Terrell had already made an impact earlier in the game, snaring a tipped Walsh pass and taking it 60 yards for a touchdown. Now here he was with 45 seconds left, lined up man to man on Miami receiver Leonard Conley, an old high school rival from Tarpon Springs High.

"As we lined up, we both had smiles on our faces, because I knew who the pass was coming to," Terrell said, "And he knew that I knew."

Instead of basking in that moment, Terrell built on it. He went on to become a first-team All-American in 1989 and was drafted in the second round by the Los Angeles Rams in the spring of 1990. His nine pro seasons included stints with the Rams, Jets, Panthers and Packers.

It was on his off-days and during the offseason that he began working on becoming a pilot.

"I gave up a lot of days on the golf course to do that," he said. "And every minute was worth it. For me it was a great thing, because a lot of people go through somewhat of a depression when they leave the NFL. I think the best thing was that I was able to walk right into a different passion of mine."

He has since started a development company on the side in Chicago, The Terrell Group, that builds commercial, residential and industrial buildings.

"I feel fortunate, because when I was a little kid, there were three things I wanted to do—play football, build buildings and fly airplanes," Terrell said. "I've gotten to do all three.

"Now football is over and the development company is just taking off. The airline industry is in a state of flux. You're not sure what's going to happen. ATA, itself, faces an uncertain future, but it's a company that's allowed me to fly all over, the world, literally to 35 countries. Now sometimes when I'm in a strange place, like Kuwait, I say, 'What in the world am I doing?' Landing is Kosovo was an experience, too. And 9/11 changed aviation forever. It was just a horrible day for our country.

"But I'm doing what I always dreamed of doing, doing what I promised my grandpa, Grady Terrell Sr., I'd do someday. And I'm loving every minute of it."

Where Have You Gone?

ROBIN WEBER

E very year for a couple of weeks at a time, Robin Weber leaves civilization with only a backpack, a fishing rod and a desire to cleanse his mind and body.

"It's kind of a Zen thing for me," said Weber, a tight end for the Notre Dame football team in the mid-'70s who now owns his own real estate company. "I go to Alaska, South America, to Alpine lakes 12-13,000 feet above sea level. I call it my yearly attitude adjustment. I go where the people aren't and where the fish are. I fish and I fast. It's a real cleansing. I mean, I don't even take booze."

On a rare chance Weber does cross paths with another human being, there's little chance they'll know who he is. The same was true, however, when Weber walked crowded city streets or even across the Notre Dame campus for most of the past three decades.

"I was just kind of languishing," said the tall Texan, who hasn't lost his drawl or his sense of humor. "Basically I had been relegated to a trivia question."

Which is a step above where his buddies Steve Neece, Steve Sylvester, Gerry DiNardo, Frank Pomarico, Mike Fanning, Kevin Nosbusch, Jim Stock, and Mark Brenneman—the Irish standouts in the trenches during that era—had been largely relegated to.

"Those guys don't get any ink, and they really deserve it," Weber said.

Weber still isn't convinced he deserves ink or face time, but he is gladly eating up the celebrity that has been afforded him the past couple of years.

The 30th anniversary celebration of Notre Dame's 1973 Sugar Bowl victory over Alabama and its national championship helped dust off Weber's heroics that season. A couple of articles in *Blue & Gold Illustrated* followed, highlighting the

#91

ROBIN WEBER

TIGHT END

PLAYING YEARS:
1973-74, 1976

CLAIM TO FAME:
Caught a 35-yard pass
from Tom Clements to
help Notre Dame
secure a Sugar Bowl
victory over Alabama,
giving the Irish the
1973 national title

HIGH SCHOOL:
Jesuit High

HOMETOWN:
Dallas, Texas

PROFESSION:
Co-owner of Weber
Commercial Real
Estate Services

**CURRENTLY RESIDES
IN:**
Chicago, Illinois

historical significance of Weber's 35-yard pass reception in the 24-23 upending of No. 1 Alabama.

Suddenly Weber's world began to change.

"I started getting letters, all kinds of requests," Weber said. "People would send me pictures from that game that they wanted autographed—pictures I didn't even know were out there.

"I said I need to parlay this into some fun, and I did. It travels around business circles now and works in my direction and opens doors that way. It also opens some other doors, too—like to the bars. I know a couple where I can drink free beer all night long."

Weber's catch was one of a multitude of big plays by the Irish on New Year's Eve, 1973 in New Orleans in the first ever meeting between college football giants Alabama and Notre Dame and coaching legends-in-the-making Bear Bryant and Ara Parseghian.

Notre Dame's Al Hunter had returned a kickoff for a touchdown 93 yards. Bob Thomas had booted the go-ahead field goal from 19 yards out with 4:26 to go in the game after missing two attempts earlier in the game.

Alabama had its spectacular and timely plays, too, and seemingly the most momentous was delivered by Crimson Tide punter Greg Gantt. On fourth-and-20, Gantt boomed a punt that settled inside the Irish five-yard line.

Weber's recollection had the ball being downed at the three. The Alabama archives say it was the two. Notre Dame's account of the game had the Irish taking possession on their own one. Tom Pagna, an offensive assistant coach for the Irish in that era, confirmed it was indeed the two.

However, Notre Dame freshman Ross Browner was flagged for roughing the punter. In those days, the penalty was 15 yards, but there was no automatic first down that came with it—something the TV announcers doing the game didn't realize. In fact, because of the announcers' misstatements, Bryant was barraged with thousands of letters and telegrams criticizing his judgment and questioning his sanity in the weeks and months that followed the game.

In reality, the penalty would have only given Alabama a fourth-and-five and still on the wrong side of the 50. Bryant opted to try to let his defense win the game.

Weber wasn't on the field for first or second down. The Irish netted a total of six yards on those two plays, bringing up third-and-four from the 8. Into the game came Weber, whose playing time for the run-oriented Irish had increased significantly from midseason on, when Notre Dame started using two-tight end sets with regularity.

Parseghian called for a running play initially, but he also wanted a long count to try to draw Alabama offsides. An Alabama defender did jump, but so did Notre Dame All-America tight end Dave Casper. Notre Dame was penalized half the distance to the goal, and the Irish were now facing a third-and-eight.

"I'm thinking now we're definitely passing," Weber said. "I kept looking over to the sideline for [split end] Pete Demmerle to come back in the game."

And for good reason. Weber, a sophomore, had caught only one pass to that point in his collegiate career. But he stayed in, and Parseghian called "tackle trap pass left."

It was a misdirection play that is designed to look like a sweep. The ball was supposed to go to Casper, according to Pagna.

Alabama loaded up nine players on the line of scrimmage, anticipating the run. Weber fired off the line and the defensive end barely touched him. The cornerback, who was supposed to be covering Weber man to man, tried to avoid Weber when the big tight end dipped his shoulder, faking that he was going to throw a block.

"I ended up just blowing right by him," Weber said. "That left only the safety, and he was giving me a huge cushion. I'm thinking to myself that maybe I should break my route off or a run a seven-yard out instead. But I remembered that I'd get in trouble, so I broke it off at 30 yards just like I was supposed to. I kept thinking, 'I hope they see me, because nobody's around me.'"

Casper was covered, and quarterback Tom Clements spotted Weber. Weber didn't immediately see the ball coming, because a defensive lineman leaped up and almost tipped the pass.

"I'm like, 'Yeeoww, here it comes,'" Weber recalled. "I caught it clean over my shoulder. I got about five more yards after the catch before the safety came over and cut me, knocking me about seven yards into the Alabama bench, right in front of Bear Bryant.

"I was laying on my back thinking, 'Am I going to be cleated?' I come out of the crowd and looked for the flag. No flag. Checkmate. Game over."

The completion gave the Irish a fresh set of downs, allowing them to run out the clock. Weber spent the rest of the game on the sidelines, then quickly left the stadium.

"I wasn't at the awards ceremony," he said. "I was like, 'Let's go down to Bourbon Street and have some fun, because it's New Year's Eve, and it was just time to do that.' I kept thinking this is what I went to college for—a great education and a chance to get a ring."

Weber didn't grow up a Notre Dame fan. The standout at Dallas's Jesuit High School was bent on attending Texas, Arkansas or Oklahoma until Notre Dame's first couple of bowl trips since the mid-'20s opened his eyes and his mind. Notre Dame officials lifted their self-imposed bowl ban in 1969, and the Irish tangled with powerful Texas teams in back-to-back seasons on New Year's Day of 1970 and '71.

"That got me started following Ara Parseghian," Weber said. "Catholic schools in the Bible Belt during that time really were looked down upon, but I think it's because the other schools were afraid to lose to them."

Weber's catch didn't transform his career, in part because of circumstance. Two of the greatest tight ends in Irish football history—Casper at the beginning of it and Ken MacAfee at the end—limited his opportunities. Injuries played into it, too.

Bones spurs were discovered in Weber's neck prior to the 1975 season. That required surgery and wiped out his season.

"I could walk, but I couldn't feel myself walk," he said. "I'd get these electric shocks from the top of my head to the bottom of my feet. It was pretty creepy. But the whole point of the surgery was for me to play football again. I was hoping I'd actually get a shot at the pros."

A knee injury in 1976 ended any thoughts of that. Weber graduated and immediately got into sales. He sold industrial supplies and over-the-road trailers until real estate caught his fancy in the mid-1980s.

In 1989, he opened his own company, which he now runs with his younger brother, Todd—Weber Commercial Real Estate Services Inc.

The original office is still in Dallas, but Robin Weber opened a Chicago office in 2004, which is where he now resides—at least 10 months of the year.

"I head to Dallas for two months when it gets below zero up here," he said. "I mean, I didn't take *that* many shots to the head."

And he has no regrets, even if his latent fame starts to fade again.

"I think every kid who plays college football wants a shot at the pros," Weber said. "But after having those two operations so close together, I figured if I kept going with my football, I'd be walking funny when I'm 50."

"Well, I'm 50 years old, and I don't walk funny. My knee doesn't hurt. My neck doesn't hurt. Life is good."

Celebrate the Variety of Notre Dame and American Sports in These Other New Releases from Sports Publishing!

Gerry Faust's Tales from the Notre Dame Sideline
by Gerry Faust, John Heisler, and Bob Logan

• 5.5 x 8.25 hardcover • 200 pages
• photos throughout
• $19.95 • (2004 release)

Riding with the Blue Moth
by Bill Hancock

• 6 x 9 hardcover
• 256 pages
• photos throughout
• $24.95

The Fighting Irish Football Encyclopedia: Third Edition
by Michael R. Steele

• 8.5 x 11 hardcover
• 530 pages
• photos throughout
• $39.95 • (2003 release)

Mike Ditka: Reflections on the 1985 Bears
by Mike Ditka with Rick Telander

• 5.5 x 8.25 hardcover
• 200 pages
• photos throughout
• $19.95

Digger Phelps's Tales from the Notre Dame Hardwood
by Digger Phelps with Tim Bourret

• 5.5 x 8.25 hardcover
• 200 pages
• photos throughout
• $19.95 • (2004 release)

The Holyfield Way: What I Learned from Evander
by Jim Thomas with commentary by Evander Holyfield

• 6 x 9 hardcover • 256 pages
• eight-page photo insert
• $24.95

Monica Brant's Secrets to Staying Fit and Loving Life
by Monica Brant

• 7 x 9 trade paper
• 192 pages
• photos throughout
• $24.95

Lost in the Sun: The Incredible True Odyssey of Roy Gleason
by Wallace Wasinack with Mark Langill

• 6 x 9 hardcover
• 256 pages
• photos throughout
• $24.95

Gene Keady: The Truth and Nothing But the Truth
by Gene Keady with Jeff Washburn

• 6 x 9 hardcover
• 250 pages
• photo insert
• $24.95

Ferdie Pacheco: Blood in My Coffee
by Ferdie Pacheco

• 6 x 9 hardcover
• 256 pages
• photo insert
• $24.95

All books are available in bookstores everywhere!
Order 24-hours-a-day by calling toll-free **1-877-424-BOOK (2665).**
Also order online at **www.SportsPublishingLLC.com.**